Bertrand Russell
A Psychobiography of a Moralist

Bertrand Russell
A Psychobiography of a Moralist

Andrew Brink

HUMANITIES PRESS INTERNATIONAL, INC.
Atlantic Highlands, NJ

First published in 1989 by
Humanities Press International, Inc.,
Atlantic Highlands, NJ 07716.

Library of Congress Cataloging-in-Publication Data

Brink, Andrew.
    Bertrand Russell, a psychobiography of a
    moralist/Andrew Brink.
       p.   cm.
    Bibliography: p.
    Includes index.
    ISBN 0–391–03600–9 : $39.95 (est.)   0–391–03605–X
    (pbk)
    1. Russell, Bertrand, 1872–1970. 2.
    Philosophers—England—Biography. I. Title.
    B1649.R94B75 1989
    192—dc 19
    [B]
                                    88–12276
                                        CIP

Printed in the United States of America

Contents

1	Introduction	1
2	Beginnings: Loss, Depression, and Creativity	15
3	Reconstructing Meaning: "The Pilgrimage of Life" and Other Early Writings	35
4	A Pathway Found: Russell's Conversion of 1901	61
5	A Pathway Lost? The Problem of Mysticism	81
6	Romantic Attachments and Illusions: Love Letters	95
7	The Angry Pacifist	113
8	Bertrand Russell's Sexual Politics	133
9	Conclusion	153
	Select Bibliography	163
	Index	171

Acknowledgments

I wish to thank McMaster University and The Social Sciences and Humanities Research Council of Canada for the research time which made possible acquaintance with the contents of the Bertrand Russell Archives and other sources of Russell's life and thought.

Earlier versions of several chapters appeared in the following journals: chapter 2 in *Mosaic* XV/1 (Winter, 1982); chapters 3 and 7 in *The Journal of Psychohistory* 10, 3 (Winter, 1983) and 12, 4 (Spring, 1985); chapters 4 and 5 in *Russell: the Journal of the Bertrand Russell Archives*, New Series 4, no. 1 (Summer, 1984) and New Series 7, no. 1 (Summer, 1987); chapter 6 in *Queen's Quarterly* (Spring, 1979).

Permissions to quote materials in the copyright of The Bertrand Russell Archives at McMaster University and The Humanities Research Center, University of Texas at Austin, were originally obtained for those articles.

I should like to thank Helen Brink for her assistance with the preparation of this book and especially for the co-authorship of chapter 8. Drs. Kenneth S. Adam, Paul Grof, and John R. Roy of the Department of Psychiatry, McMaster University Medical Centre, supported my efforts to understand Russell psychobiographically. Discussions of papers given at conferences of The International Psychohistorical Association in New York City brought further clarification. David Holbrook of Downing College, Cambridge, has been unfailingly helpful, as have my students Maria Forte and George Johnson.

CHAPTER

1

Introduction

"Men are passionate, headstrong and rather mad."
—Russell, *Human Society in Ethics and Politics*

Bertrand Russell was among this century's most provocative and contentious commentators on human relations. Not only did he assess and pronounce upon every political and social development in a highly unstable era, he set out to reform the very basis of human relations in male-female sexuality, in marriage, and in parenthood. Known first as a logician and philosopher of the most severely analytic sort, Russell turned his formidable talents toward being a prophet in human affairs. A brilliant essayist and publicist, Russell became as insistent a voice for sexual reform as he had been for remaking philosophy at the beginning of the century. What were the main factors leading to his wish to overturn centuries of Christian insistence on married monogamy, on fidelity in marriage? Can the Russell who had four wives and many affairs be explained in terms other than the social forces shaping him? To what extent was he himself a shaper of changes that have permanently altered our view of human relations? A virulent antagonist to most religious claims, Russell sought new ethical foundations to replace absolute religious standards. A psychobiographical study of the formation of Russell's personality can be attempted for two main reasons: because most of the enormous accumulation of his archives, including private correspondence, is open to research, and because developments in psychodynamic theory, especially in "attachment theory," help make Russell's early life material intelligible in ways it never was before.

Russell is unusual in being a moralist and crusader for social

1

change for whom ethics was relativistic, incapable of being founded on indubitable first principles. He discovered himself to be philosophically incapable of an objective ethics. An attempt in *The Problems of Philosophy* (1912), challenged by Santayana in *Winds of Change*, left Russell having to say that something was good or bad only because we feel it to be so. Much as he wanted to assert, for instance, that killing in war is evil, no rational system permitted this statement. In *Human Society in Ethics and Politics* (1954) he struggled with the problem of evil, saying that "an ethical judgment does not state a fact; it states . . . some hope or fear, some desire or aversion, some love or hate."[1] The most the rationalist can offer is

> an ethic by which desires may be distinguished as right or wrong, or, speaking loosely, as good or bad. Right desires will be those that are capable of being compossible with as many other desires as possible; wrong desires will be those that can only be satisfied by thwarting other desires.[2]

Higher ethical desires presumably would be thwarted by baser ones even in a life "inspired by love and guided by knowledge," as he wrote in "What I Believe."[3] But how is one to know whether desires are of a high or a base sort if they spring from an unanalyzed impulse to "love"? In Russell's thinking, moral obligation is subject to shifting psychological states, with matters of conscience in interpersonal relations difficult to be sure about. Of one thing he was sure: there had been too much dwelling on "sin," and a different direction had to be found. Brought up in a puritanical Victorian ambience, Russell was looking for release from the pervasive bad conscience fostered by his grandmother and those around her at Pembroke Lodge. We will see that for Russell the meanings of "desire" and "good and bad" in relationships, including the sexual, were exceedingly problematic. His formal statements about them seem inadequate in view of his actual life experiences, perhaps mainly because Russell's psychology of desire was rudimentary and the passions which drove him were so relentless. For this reason it is well to look into the developmental origins of Russell's moralizing to ask what persuaded him to come forward as a prophet both of international peace and of revised standards of sexual morality. We shall seek motives for the radicalism which helped to dislocate values that had long been held inviolable in Western society. At the same time Russell helped to establish new values—saying "no" to nuclear war, and "yes" to sexual freedoms. Both need elucidating because the implicit connection of love and war in Russell's mind offers a key to the moral puzzle of human destructiveness.

A further assertion of this study is that Russell was never the rationalist he wanted to be. An intellectual descendant of Francis Bacon, the thought-reforming Renaissance essayist, of the skeptical philosophers Descartes and Hume, and of the empiricists Locke and Mill, Russell thought of himself as a prophet of reason, not a latter-day romantic. Belief in the power of intellect to settle all questions is present not only throughout Russell's philosophical writings but also in those on social questions. Russell stands more as a skeptical assailant of outmoded belief systems than as a builder of new ones. Typically, he thought better of Descartes's method of doubt than of his subsequent theory of knowledge. On the level of social theory Russell could never firmly settle on an affiliation:

> I have imagined myself in turn, a Liberal, a Socialist, or a Pacifist, but I have never been any of these things, in any profound sense. Always the skeptical intellect, when I have most wished it silent, has whispered doubts to me, has cut me off from the facile enthusiasms of others, and has transported me into a desolate solitude.[4]

In other words, doubts could both stifle ideals and cripple affiliative wishes. Why Russell's pervasive doubts? Why the unrelieved sense of aloneness and mistrust of moral and political systems? And why was Russell so attracted to thinkers such as Descartes who so relentlessly separated reason from emotion? The present study examines the affective dimension of Russell's skeptical intellect, the hidden but discoverable states of feeling that pushed him toward the artifice of placing reason over emotion.

For Russell reason seems to have been as much a defense against affect as it was a tool of attack upon aspects of thought, belief, and social practice he disliked or mistrusted. But from what did the weapon of intellect give protection? Was Russell sheltering from the claims of emotion, engendered by his upbringing, that he could not meet? Was it specifically the excessive claims upon him by caretaking women? We shall see that Russell's chief substitute parent, his paternal grandmother, had much to do with both frustrating him morally and honing his intellect to an uncommon sharpness. As he wrote at age sixteen in "Greek Exercises," "*The* great inducement to a good life with me is Granny's love, and the immense pain I know it gives her when I go wrong."[5] Her role in forming an excessively guilty, yet rebellious, conscience will be examined. On the other side of the family, that of his Grandmother Stanley, the exercise of intellect at age eighteen may be glimpsed in a vignette of the evening company at Dover Street discussing Home Rule.[6] The role of formidably controlling intellectual women in Russell's early life has not had the emphasis it deserves. The exercise of intellect became a prime technique in surviving among them, yet the early confessional diaries show more of the doubting, questioning inner self confronting such mysteries as Christian belief in immortality. Tenuously joined reason and emotion are present at the start of Russell's self-recorded life: they seem to be part of an obsessive safeguard against potentially catastrophic depressive mood change.

As philosopher, Russell's excursion into pure reason appears to have been less satisfactory than he had hoped, although the nonspecialist is unable to make a fair assessment of what was actually accomplished. Russell changed the direction of twentieth-century philosophy; yet one asks how his attempt to see mathematics as a more highly developed form of logic could be anything other than depersonalized. Had not this been his attraction to mathematics from the start—that it was not human? In "The Study of Mathematics" (1907) Russell wrote an apologia for the impersonal beauty of number: "Mathematics, rightly viewed, possesses not only truth, but supreme beauty—a beauty cold and austere, like that of sculpture, without appeal to any part of our weaker nature . . ."; and he continues, "Real life is, to most men, a long second-best, a perpetual compromise between the ideal and the possible; but the world of pure reason knows no compromise, no practical limitations."[7] Mathematics is commended as being "remote from human passions," "the region of absolute necessity"; and so it was that Russell first sought to overcome a human world governed by fate and suffering.[8] It sounds like psychiatric jargon to label this schizoid isolation, but that is what it remained until after expending his best intellectual efforts on mathematical logic, Russell worked his way back into the human world and an engagement with its problems of relationship. As he explains in "The Retreat from Pythagoras" (1959), the Great War forced a change: "All the high-flown thoughts that I had had about the abstract world of ideas seemed to me thin and rather trivial in view of the vast suffering that surrounded me. The non-human world remained as an occasional refuge, but not as a country in which to build one's permanent habitation."[9] The Platonic vision of mathematics "has come to seem to me largely nonsense, partly for technical reasons and partly from a change in my general outlook upon the world. Mathematics has ceased to seem to me non-human in its subject-matter. I have come to believe, though very reluctantly, that it consists of tautologies."[10] And we are told that "I no longer have the wish to thrust out human elements from regions where they belong; I have no longer the feeling that intellect is superior to sense."[11] This transformation took several decades, and it needs to be understood in the context of Russell's "conversion" of 1901, his first major acknowledgment that human life is subject to powerfully repressed emotions. Had more self-therapeutic use been made of this remarkable event, Russell's human relationships might not have been so perilous. Here it is enough to say that changed emphases in the psycho-social study of personality prompt us to ask about the events leading Russell from Platonism to realism and to the sort of social commitment he attempted. Was his social commitment contaminated by the psychological residues of an unhappy childhood from which escape into mathematics had failed to deliver him? Is it also true that his commitment to peace, and to a more just social order, is attributable to depressive childhood suffering? If so these positive outcomes of broken attachments may be accounted for.

Psychobiographical enquiry into such questions may still seem an impertinence. I believe, however, that because Russell launched a frontal attack on the Western value system governing love and marriage, his reasons for doing so should be scrutinized. As he challenged the time honored institution of monogamy in the name of a kind of hedonism, so should we challenge him to answer for the changes he wanted. That Russell was willing to have his psychology and his private life studied is certain from the ample records he left behind. Not only are there three volumes of *Autobiography* containing many private letters, but the collections from which they were extracted have been preserved for use by researchers. Much little-known confessional and related material appears in the recently edited *Cambridge Essays, 1888–99* and *Contemplation and Action, 1902–14*, the first two volumes in the non-technical series of *The Collected Papers of Bertrand Russell*. Intensive work as an editor of these materials fundamentally changed my view of Russell. To annotate and introduce papers it was necessary to read hundreds of unpublished letters from which a picture emerged differing even from the *Autobiography*. Disturbing features of the relational life showed that Russell's biography needs reformulation from a psychological point of view. What are the problems toward which the present study turns?

The chief difficulty in thinking about Russell the social and sexual reformer is the discrepancy between his high-minded ethical aims—for instance in assisting the Suffrage Movement—and the cruel outcomes of his marriages and Don Juan adventures. Russell manipulated and hurt women, such as his first wife Alys and his lover Helen Dudley, who placed trust in him. Women on intimate terms with him sooner or later experienced his fierce revolt against conventional mating. In 1932 he confided in Lady Ottoline Morrell that "there must be something wrong about me, as I seem to be always hurting the people I am fondest of, and quite inadvertently" (29 January 1932, #1702). As his estranged wife Dora saw it, Russell was quite callous about his separations. She wrote that after years of marriage, children, and cooperation at Beacon Hill School, his leaving her for Patricia Spence brought her up against "a blank wall of indifference so complete as to seem hardly conceivable."[12] Her general comment is:

> He could passionately and romantically "fall in love," with so deep a devotion that he could not live without the beloved; but he was able, should a new love come his way, so completely to set aside the old one as almost to forget her existence and her very nature.[13]

Were Russell's changes of lovers, which with age came to be seen as philandering habits, purely a private matter, or do they bear on his public pronouncements about human relations? Surely Russell's ambivalent love-hate of women has to be taken into account when looking back on his crusade for sexual freedoms; more than social factors such as contraceptives and the automobile were involved. Yet such insights should not disqualify Russell as a social prophet, however much they prevent taking at face value all he said. Russell sincerely wanted a better world—one freed of cant and hypocrisy, of intolerance and persecution, of injustice and war. From as early as *The Principles of Social Reconstruction* (1916) he organized a program to promote human creativity while ridding the world of conflict and war. Where he went wrong was in simplifying human nature, in wishful thinking about progressive possibilities apart from a radical critique of how individuals develop in the maternal, familial, and social nexuses. Too much a nineteenth-century progressivist, Russell failed to notice that the social sciences, and especially psychoanalysis, would force a revision of how we look upon the possibilities of human fulfilment, individually and in groups. His public optimism about human nature, unwarranted in the form it took, needs reconsidering against the background of his obsessive destructiveness in relationships. Russell's depressiveness made him acutely sensitive to human suffering on the large scale, but his controlling, competitive, obsessional defense, when used in more proximal relations, whether in winning arguments or leaving intimate relations with women, inflicted cruelties he could never explain. We are in a much better position to do so.

Can reliable psychobiography be written, even for so well documented a figure as Russell? While nothing definitive should be claimed, surely a beginning can be made. Psychologically informed individual life-history is gaining ground as the study of human development improves, and its implications for literary and biographical inquiry are being understood. Caution as to methodology and extent of claims should be exercised, as William McKinley Runyan urges in *Life Histories and Psychobiography: Explorations in Theory and Method* (1982). A clinical psychologist, Runyan is especially concerned that balanced use be made of early childhood material, and stresses that psychoanalysis is no longer bounded by Freudian theory alone. Newer, more empirical studies in human development improve the reliability of assessing inner states and behaviors over a lifetime. Well documented retrospective studies of important personages have the advantage of seeing the life in its stages and at its completion, even without actual interviews with the subject.

The rigorous critique of Freudianism, especially by W. R. D. Fairbairn and Harry Guntrip in Britain, opened a new phase of psychobiographical and critical possibility. The first to show the pertinence of this view of human nature to literary study was the Cambridge critic David Holbrook, in *Human Hope and the Death Instinct* (1971) and elsewhere. While the present study does not engage in theoretical discussions, nor even make as much of the "schizoid diagnosis" of Russell's deep subjectivity as it might, its orientation is to object-relations theory, as supplemented by psychobiographical attachment theory. Debates are inevitable about which theories alternative to Freud's are relevant to a given subject matter, and of course theory is itself in constant change. Developmental studies of early child attachment and loss by John Bowlby are replacing drive theory with experimentally verifiable descriptions of maternal attachment essential for the healthy growth of each new being. The implications for later psychological styles of kinds and qualities of initial attachment and loss of attachment are beginning to be recognized. Bowlby's attachment theory is used in these chapters as giving a firm starting point for explaining Russell's depressive reaction to the early deaths of his parents. I am persuaded that Bowlby's work has enough acceptance to use it in deciding the meaning of Russell's "tragic" sense of life and the compensatory "religion of beauty" offered to those who feel "exiles on an inhospitable shore."[14] That Russell was ego weakened and had a lifelong apprehension of loss will appear in these pages. In discussing the problem of the obsessional style of defending the ego—which lies beyond Bowlby's theories—I draw upon papers by the New York psychoanalyst Matthew Besdine, less well attested but pointing the way to further research into the origins of sexual ambivalence and the inability to form lasting attachments.

I am aware that the attempt to do psychobiography is perilous, and that a bad one is worse than none at all. A beginning must nonetheless be made to test developmental theory and to elucidate the mystery of high creativity such as Russell's. Could it be that his early creative writings such as *The Pilgrimage of Life* (1902–3) and "The Free Man's Worship" (1903) were the start of a venture in psychological "repair" that was overwhelmed by misguided intellectualism? Did Russell make discoveries in *Prisons* (1911) and *The Perplexities of John Forstice* (1912) about what William James had called "the divided self" that, had he been able to follow through on them, would have more completely validated his humanitarianism? In this sense, Russell's supreme powers as a mathematical logician may have played him false by leading into realms of abstraction instead of following guidance of a healthier sort that would have made him a great psychological novelist or a psychological theoretician in his own right. But Russell was short on the imaginative gifts for empathetic characterization that make a novelist such as Tolstoy; nor did he possess the "psychological mindedness" of a James or a Freud. The irresistible temptation to intellectual omnipotence gradually eroded Russell's reserves of imaginative creativity. His short stories *Satan in the Suburbs* (1953) and *Nightmares of Eminent Persons* (1954), which won little critical acclaim, read as contrivances rather than as fruitions of the writer's inner necessity. Russell was much more comfortable as a "thinker" and as a publicist for reform. He worked on the dangerous boundary between the incontrovertible personal authority of the Victorian sage, as he admired in Thomas Carlyle, and the humbler pursuits of those whose minds were formed after the messages of William James, Freud, John B. Watson, and Havelock Ellis (Russell's main psychological mentors) had been absorbed into the culture. Russell's clarity of argumentation and his lucid prose style allowed him to simplify social matters that would prove much more problematic than he could allow. His pronouncements on human behavior often seem ill founded, or the products of wishful thinking brilliantly presented with an aristocrat's aplomb. Initially Russell's writing on love and sexuality seems to have enjoyed much public acceptance. What reader of his popular essays would think that so seemingly confident a writer might be trying to solve problems of his own? Only by beginning with his earliest, unsteady efforts at creative writing does the meaning of his literary quest appear. It begins to be possible to explain a need for imaginative repair which failed fully to materialize. But to speak of imaginative failure should not cause us to forget the most important humane legacy Russell left—the autobiographical record, including letters, of his struggle for psychological integration. It is a record set against a background of socio-political conflict upon which he was often a brilliantly incisive commentator.

Psychobiography is a new sort of endeavor, whose findings cannot be called fully objective. The problem of introducing one's own subjectivity into a psychobiographical reconstruction must be faced. No doubt all biography is in some degree the autobiography of its maker, and the biographer's reasons for attraction to his subject have a lot to do with what he finds. I cannot pretend to a dispassionate concern with Russell, whose thought more than that of any other has helped me to organize my sense of social and moral change. At the same time I see that his social and psychological thought have often been misjudged and require reconsideration along biographical lines. If Russell's motives for social criticism and corrective action were not always what he said or implied, biographical rather than ideological clarifications should be attempted. The debate over Russell's feminism, for instance, needs as its starting point a clear account of what Russell really felt about women, and why he felt it. Not only the interpersonal background of attitudes, but its psychogenesis, needs accounting for. When, as early as *The Principles of Social Reconstruction* (1916), Russell campaigned for "creative" as opposed to "possessive" sexual and marital relationships, we should see both an extension of liberal ideology and evidences of personal need requiring explanation. Did Russell hurt the cause of women as much as he helped it? He certainly wielded a two-edged sword of both hurting and helping, whose effects need accounting for when the story of the changing status of women in the twentieth century is being told. Ideally the biographer would try to plot his own position in this debate, not pretending to immunity from the issues, however much his time and circumstances differ from those of his subject. For my own part, like Alan Wood as long ago as 1957, I think that Russell was "incapable of understanding the arguments for conventional marriage," although better reasons for this incapacity can now be found.[15] Russell got most of the sexual freedoms he sought, and we, having witnessed the large-scale social consequences, may well become revisionist, asking whether Russell campaigned for new forms of emotional bondage rather than freedom.

Every biographical study can be placed on a continuum from idealization to debunking of the subject, both extremes being unrealistic. This study reflects my own emergence from late teenage idealization of Russell, who spoke for humane values to someone raised in a predominantly scientific environment. His enlightened liberalism, critique of organized religion, and pacifism all strongly appealed. Furthermore, Russell's powers as an essayist put him in the public realm as spokesman for much of what I believed. This persuasion lay behind my M.A. thesis, "A Study of the Development of Bertrand Russell's Social Criticism with Special Reference to his Essays" (1958), but I had not at that stage looked at what "development" might really mean. In England I joined the Campaign for Nuclear Disarmament and later associated with the Committee of 100, participating in demonstrations led by Russell against nuclear weapons. To an as yet uncynical student generation, Russell the octogenarian spoke for hope in a world darkened by the possibility of extinction in nuclear war. The alternatives he posed were stark and clear: "Shall we put an end to the human race; or shall mankind renounce war?", as he had written in a magnificently trenchant statement, "Man's Peril" (1955).[16] Yet we did not know much about Russell, about the man and his conflicts with authority having a history as far back as the Boer War, not to mention the pacifist heroics of the Great War of 1914. The group mind was turned toward Russell's warnings here and now, unaware of the reasons for the extremes to which he, and the Committee of 100, would go in discomfiting the government of the day.

In 1979 I helped to form the plans which resulted in the McMaster edition of *The Collected Papers of Bertrand Russell*, based on archival holdings in the university. This scheme had brave beginnings, and I entered fully into them. Editing some of Russell's early essays and other writings, as they appear in volumes 1 and 12, brought a privileged acquaintance with much more biographical data than had been worked with before. The psychobiographer could not hope for a better guide to recurrent emotive themes and conflicts than Russell's vast personal correspondence, especially with the women he loved, tried to love, and left. Reading Russell's private correspondence revealed a depth of psychological torment quite at odds with his performance as a rational thinker. A Russell emerged for whom I was not entirely prepared even by the *Autobiography*, and I found it impossible to take him at the level of his published statements alone. Ronald W. Clark's *The Life of Bertrand Russell* (1975) had rather sensationalized Russell's amours but without satisfactorily explaining them. I wanted something more psychologically convincing than conventional biography could supply.

Editing has become a sort of pseudo-science, with its own dogmas of dispassionate objectivity, extending even to footnotes, headnotes, and introductions to collected papers. In a group-editing endeavor distinctive points of view must give way to the honorifics which it is assumed the consumer-users of the product want. The huge monetary investment in academic editing requires that products be in every respect above reproach. This turns the humanist used to working with ideas and feelings into a technician faced with having to falsify his perceptions. For example, there was little leeway in handling the "confessional" materials, including journals of the most self-revealing sort published in volumes 1 and 12 of the *Collected Papers*. To keep the edition as value-free as possible, interpretations of such materials were discouraged, yet it is especially from them that renewed interest in Russell is emerging. This was particularly difficult for me, since I had become acquainted with post-Freudian psychodynamic theory and had learned to view depression and suicidal ideation in a framework of attachment behavior. Such ideas were, of course, alien to Russell, but they began to make sense of what was plainly visible in the genesis of his creativity. Unfortunately my changing views of Russell's thought and teaching proved to be incompatible with dominant views in the editorial group. The present study attempts to do more justice by Russell's early personal writings than was possible in editing them. The chapters grew incrementally with the editing, and they benefited from many discussions with colleagues in the Department of Psychiatry, psychohistorians, and others informed about the psychodynamic principles being used.

A new perspective on Russell's contributions in forming late-twentieth-century liberal awareness is needed. I hope that this study will make Russell seem more humanly significant and approachable than can the intellectualist treatment of his work enshrined in the *Collected Papers*. The helpful and harmful meanings of his creativity are far too important to leave to academic image making. Russell once wrote a pair of essays called "Ideas That Have Helped Mankind" and "Ideas That Have Harmed Mankind," no doubt realizing that his own "ideas" would similarly be weighed. Do we have a better balanced instrument with which to weigh the feelings in ideas? As he himself said, ideas are inseparable from passions:

> I think that the evils that men inflict on each other, and by reflection upon themselves, have their main source in evil passions rather than in ideas or beliefs.[17]

Notes

1. Bertrand Russell, *Human Society in Ethics and Politics* (London: Allen & Unwin, 1954), p. 25.
2. Ibid., p. 59.
3. Russell, *Why I Am Not a Christian* (London: Allen & Unwin, 1957), p. 44.
4. Russell, *Autobiography, Vol II, 1914–44* (Toronto: McClelland and Stewart, 1968), p. 38.
5. Russell, *Cambridge Essays, 1888–99*, ed. K. Blackwell, et al., *The Collected Papers of Bertrand Russell*, Vol. 1 (London: Allen & Unwin, 1983), p. 15.
6. Ibid., pp. 54–55.
7. Russell, *Contemplation and Action, 1902–14*, ed. R. A. Rempel et al., *Collected Papers*, Vol. 12 (London: Allen & Unwin, 1985), p. 86.
8. Ibid., pp. 86, 91.
9. Russell, *My Philosophical Development* (London: Unwin Paperbacks, 1985), p. 157.
10. Ibid., p. 157.
11. Ibid., p. 158.
12. Dora Russell, *The Tamarisk Tree: My Quest for Liberty and Love* (London: Elek/Pemberton, 1975), p. 247.
13. Ibid., p. 245.
14. Russell, *Autobiography, Vol. I, 1872–1914* (Toronto: McClelland and Stewart, 1967), pp. 85, 98, 187.

15. Alan Wood, *Bertrand Russell: The Passionate Sceptic* (London: Allen & Unwin, 1957), p. 171.
16. Russell, *Portraits from Memory* (London: Allen & Unwin, 1956), p. 217.
17. Russell, *Unpopular Essays* (London: Allen & Unwin, 1950), p. 189.

2

Beginnings: Loss, Depression, and Creativity

"I suffered before I began to think: which is the common fate
of man, though crueller in my case than in another's."
—Rousseau, *Confessions*

Remembering his school days in 1888, Bertrand Russell wrote in his
Autobiography of the footpath at Southgate: "I used to go there alone to
watch the sunset and contemplate suicide. I did not, however, commit suicide, because I wished to know more of mathematics."[1]
Although this statement clearly links Russell's creativity with death-
oriented anxieties, biographers have tended to overlook the extent to
which a "loss-repair" theory is essential for an understanding of his
genius.

According to the loss-repair theory, creativity is a natural psy-
chobiological control placed upon the risk of loss-caused depressive
affect emerging disturbingly into consciousness. "You create out of
what you lack. Not what you have," writes the novelist John Fowles.[2]
In this view creativity begins with an ego deficit, not a surplus. Thus
artistic and intellectual creativity may be a defensive procedure in
which the created object becomes a source of gratification as a "new
thing"—a poem, a math solution, a sculpture—drawing upon, but
not acknowledging, a basic ego conflict. But creativity can further be
an ego reparative procedure in which threatening feelings of loss are
measured out to the self in symbolic ways that help to integrate and
reduce their threat. By a sort of leakage from the ego the creative
person receives for inclusion in his symbolic compositions the uncon-

scious conflicted material that, were it encountered all at once, might overwhelm him. This material is transformed and stabilized in formal compositions.

The loss-repair theory also allows the possibility that the recreation of lost attachment objects may be carried out in actual human attachments, though there is danger that these will be maladaptive if awareness of what they mean is lacking. Self-monitoring to promote reparative good relationships depends on what is learned from the sort of creativity which gives access to conflicted feelings; the non-learning sort of creativity may easily be mere self-compensatory avoidance behavior. It may also, of course, lead to discovery of new truth about the world, as in scientific and mathematical research.

Russell's creativity is of both types—his work in mathematical logic tending toward the defensive type—although a rigid distinction should not be made. We are looking at what creativity means in the causes and outcomes of his actual relationships, but it is well to be reminded first of Russell's intellectual distinctions.

Russell's achievements are many. Most impressively he originated modern analytical philosophy. His *Principia Mathematica* (with A. N. Whitehead), demonstrating that classical mathematics is reducible to logic, is ranked as one of the great feats of human intellect, comparable to Sir Isaac Newton's *Principia* in the seventeenth century. In his lifetime of ninety-seven years (1872–1970) Russell wrote some seventy books of philosophy, social and political theory, and imaginative fiction, about 2,500 essays and many thousands of letters, the best of them of the highest literary quality. He was a Nobel laureate for literature, a Fellow of the Royal Society, and held the Order of Merit—acknowledgment that he was one of the great men of our time.

It may be surprising to hear that so creative a person had marked depressive features to his personality, that this rationalist and social optimist had episodes of cosmic despair, that when he toyed with the idea of suicide it was not entirely for effect, and that morbid sadness and loneliness were moods not easy to dispel.

There are reasons in Russell's early traumatic parent losses to expect an underlying depression leading to suicidal thoughts, but let us first look at the defensive tactics Russell built to deal with depressive risk, tactics which define, and in part explain, his sort of creativity. By defense is meant the learned intrapsychic tactic, with behavioral expression, by which unpleasant mood changes are guarded against. Russell's biographer, Ronald W. Clark, emphasizes the extent to which his subject was compulsively changeable in his personal relations, especially in relations with women, and he gives prominence to Russell's series of marriages and affairs. Clark, however, raises more questions than he can answer about the reasons for them because he does not see the extent to which emotional conflict drove Russell, through hope and despair of finding sustaining attachment, to love and to write as he did. The concept of the obsessional defense helps us to grasp what actually went on, since among its features is a compulsive drive, the wish to exert control over ideas and persons, together with ambivalent attachments to persons.[3]

When Russell wrote and revised his *Autobiography* (published between 1967 and 1969) he drew upon and even printed some of the love correspondence; but he did so selectively and guardedly. To be fair to him, he did his best to comply with the modern demand for "all the truth"; he had read Freud with approval, although his most serious attention to psychology was given to William James and later to the pioneer behaviorist J. B. Watson. The letters in the *Autobiography* supply supporting evidence for its narrative; but to someone reading entire sets of love correspondences the emotional highs and lows through which Russell lived seem muted in the published letters. He puts a much more rational shape to experience than it actually had, and in Volume II he admits to surprise at realizing how many "violent fluctuations" his feelings actually went through. To read his love letters is to wonder how, in the torment of ambivalent feelings, he kept going at all.

Russell is not known to have had any psychotherapy, though in 1916 he considered it with the Swiss therapist in Lausanne, Roger Vittoz, who was treating Russell's lover, Lady Ottoline Morrell.[4] Russell's main therapy came by writing, by a constant reconstruction of his life through correspondence—brilliant commentary on amorous vicissitudes and the other relational uncertainties typifying his life. The letters are "creative" products in their own right, a self-mythologizing of elation and despair that went with his search for the perfect love. Letter writing (together with long walks) seems to have kept him from the excesses of unbearable affect. Like much Romantic art, Russell's confessional letters are adaptational control systems that keep in measure the mood shifts whose dangers he feared.

Two of the great love correspondences of this century are Russell's with Lady Ottoline Morrell (between 1911 and 1938) and with Lady Constance Malleson (between 1916 and 1970), showing him driven by forces he little understood but wished to master. As he says in *Marriage and Morals* (1929), "The claims of love to a recognized place in human life are . . . very great. But love is an anarchic force which, if it is left free, will not remain within any bounds set by law or custom."[5] During one of their quarrels, Lady Ottoline wrote to Russell: "I am sure that all or nearly all the criticisms that you have against me are due to obsessions—I suppose [these] obsessions are due to past grievances."[6] She states exactly the issue I wish to examine.

Russell was four times married (never widowed); he had several affairs that came to public notice and others that did not. I take Russell's statement (cancelled from an early draft of the *Autobiography*), that he could sustain an attachment to a woman for not more than seven years, to indicate a psychological problem, although Russell himself does not put it that way, saying only that for him love must be ecstatic, ideally preferred to love as loyalty and the long habit of sharing experience. As he explains in "What I Have Lived For,"

> I have sought love, first, because it brings ecstasy—ecstasy so great that I would often have sacrificed all the rest of life for a few hours of this joy. I have sought it, next, because it relieves loneliness—that terrible loneliness in which one shivering consciousness looks over the rim of the world into the cold unfathomable lifeless abyss. I have sought it, finally, because in the union of love I have seen, in a mystic miniature, the prefiguring vision of the heaven that saints and poets have imagined.
>
> (*Autobiography* I, 13)

It may seem wrong to question so fine a statement, but I do not think that Russell's requirement of repeated ecstasy in love is realistic. This spiritual elevation seems too much to ask of ordinary human relations.

Only Russell's confession of "terrible loneliness" begins to explain the demand for an equal and opposite extreme, unitive ecstasy. Despite the success of his last marriage at age eighty, we may guess that the human incarnation of this ideal was never found. The quest for such perfection in an imperfect world more than suggests a "psychological" problem leading to creativity—leading to the creation of what he thought he lacked.

What was this problem, and why did it exist? Clark opens his biography with a section called "The Reason Why" as a prelude to the next, "The New Romantic," in which he reconstructs Russell's two most remarkable affairs, those with Lady Ottoline Morrell and Lady Constance Malleson. But Clark has no explanation for the compulsive changeableness. He says only that Russell shared with common humanity physical passions, which he had "to an abnormal degree." He notes that because of early multiple bereavement Russell understood common humanity's emotional needs. But rather than look in the aftermath of loss for the psychogenesis of a possible obsessional neurosis, Clark's explanation for Russell's tortured search for love is impotence. This view Clark takes from Russell's estranged second wife, Dora, who indeed bore him two children. Dora Russell says that at their marriage he was "dubious of ever begetting a child." "Gossip" she adds, "has put upon his alleged numerous love affairs an entirely false interpretation. I believe that he always hoped that a sufficiently strong attraction to some woman would overcome his disability by spontaneous natural means."[7] Clark thinks that perhaps impotence resulted from physical accident, not wishing to pursue the possibility that it was the result of upbringing, or of both. A further comment by Dora Russell is helpful in this connection: "I doubt if he ever experienced the full sexual thrust of the male. It was inhibited in him by his cold loveless aristocratic upbringing, and by his own intense devotion to intellect. He was a frightened small boy . . . a lonely man out in the cold without the constant physical and emotional warmth of a woman beside him."[8] "Cold loveless aristocratic upbringing" is not quite right; there was love of a kind throughout childhood as we shall see, but this explanation at least promises some reasons "why." A psychological theory about parent loss, depressive risk, and a defensive style built during successive infant caretaking attachments will help to solve the biographical problem.

Russell's father, Lord Amberley (1842–76), was the eldest son of Lord John Russell, the successful Liberal reformer and Prime Minister of England. Amberley grew up in the shadow of this eminent man. In his *Autobiography*, Russell says of his father's temperament that it was "philosophical, studious, unworldly, morose and priggish." Amberley married Kate Stanley (1842–74) of another aristocratic and highly intellectual family. Her mother, Lady Stanley of Alderley, was a founder of Girton College, Cambridge, and a non-believer. Russell describes his mother "as I came to know her . . . later from her diary and her letters, [as] vigorous, lively, witty, serious, original and fearless" (*Autobiography* I, 15). In later life Russell reconstructed as fully as he could his parents' lives from their letters and diaries—a significant reparative act. Both parents championed such radical opinions as birth-control and votes for women. There were three children: Frank (1865–1931), Rachel, the survivor of twins (1868–74), and Bertrand (1872–1970), the third Earl Russell upon succeeding Frank.

There is nothing to show that there was irregularity in Russell's mothering. He was a robust baby and, after initial adjustments, nursing went well. For at least six months, and probably longer, he was exclusively breast fed by his mother. Up to December 1873 Russell was attentively cared for by his mother, if surviving letters may be taken as a guide. But then there was a disruption when his father, mother, and brother Frank went to Italy for his father's health. Russell, aged one year and seven or eight months, and his sister Rachel were left with their grandmother and Aunt Agatha Russell at Pembroke Lodge. There was caretaking difficulty in January 1874 when a nurse, Miss Strauss, was dismissed. When Russell's grandmother became ill, his aunt Agatha took over his management. These changes could not have been beneficial.

After a six-month absence, Russell's parents returned in May. But then tragedy struck. On the journey back to England Frank developed diphtheria and recovered in London, only to be brought home to Ravenscroft in Wales while still infectious. The reunited family was thus exposed and Rachel went down with the disease. Her mother, exhausted by nursing her (as she had Frank earlier), and no doubt generally stressed by reestablishing family and household after a long absence, could not resist infection. She died of diphtheria on 28 June 1874, followed by six-year-old Rachel on 3 July. The letters in *The Amberley Papers* narrating these events have the restrained dignity and poignance of Greek tragedy. Russell's comments are similarly brief and restrained—testimony to the stoic clear-sightedness with which, as editor of the papers, he faced his past.

At age two Russell thus lost his mother and sister. Only eighteen months later he also lost his father who, never being strong, and having been weakened by grief, died of bronchial pneumonia. After a struggle for custody, in itself undoubtedly distressing to a precocious child, Russell and his elder brother were sent to live with his paternal grandparents at Pembroke Lodge in Richmond Park. Additional unsettling factors clustered in those first years. As Alan Wood explains, the year after Russell was born Amberley "had an illness which was diagnosed, probably inexpertly, as epilepsy. . . . The next year Amberley's brother William became insane, remaining so till his death in 1933."[9] The impact of this knowledge should not be underestimated. Russell was "haunted by the fear of the family ghost," which cast gloom on every relationship past and present. Awareness of the extent and seriousness of family tragedy, fear that his mother might be alive but mad, "haunting terrors of loss," and violent nightmares of being murdered—all infringed on the happiness of anticipating his first marriage.[10] Indeed he grasped at marriage for deliverance into sanity, challenging his grandmother on the point. Family mental illness led Russell's grandmother to fear it in his offspring, using this fear in her attempt to block his marriage to Alys Pearsall Smith. When Russell saw the speciousness of this tactic, he felt release from the worst terrors of family.

"'I was born unhappy,'" Alan Wood quotes Russell as writing, "calculating gloomily, when he was five, that if he lived till seventy he still had to endure all except one-fourteenth of his life."[11] The *Autobiography*, however, records that "My childhood was, on the whole, happy and straightforward. . . ."; it was in adolescence that he felt "very lonely and very unhappy" (I,38). But Russell also says that the loss of his parents mattered greatly to him, undoubtedly because his grandmother dwelt on it. Although there is no direct evidence of the effective mourning necessary to repair the worst effects of loss,[12] he does say that the very atmosphere of his grandmother's house, Pembroke Lodge, caused him to live in the past: "I wove fantasies about my parents and my sister." He admits to having "felt some kind of unhappiness, as I remember wishing that my parents had lived" (I, 19, 31). The unhappiness no doubt prompted reparative fantasies that called back his parents as much as it was possible to do. Later, the accidental destruction of his most treasured possession, a miniature of his mother, brought grief and anger against his first wife, whom he held responsible. A tenuous link to the past had been broken. We know that he sought imaginative stimulation in such writings as Walter Pater's "Imaginary Portraits"—an indication that fantasy was important to him. As he says, "the most vivid part of my [childhood] existence was solitary," spent musing in the eleven acres of garden at Pembroke Lodge (I, 30–31).[13] The young Russell was ascetic, but his later anti-asceticism is equally an outcome of this early phase of life. He reports reparative object search against a background of transience: "I used to wander about the garden, alternately collecting birds' eggs and meditating on the flight of time" (I, 20). In the "Greek Exercises" (private reflections at age sixteen) Russell writes: "It is difficult not to become reckless and commit suicide, which I believe I should do but for my people" (I, 55). There are several later restatements of this possible way out of difficulty, making us aware that the phrase "but for my people" may have been a more significant deterrent than at first seems, a genuine protective factor, despite the gloom they cast.

There is more to Russell's creativity than attempted symbolic repair of parent loss. Maternal deprivation in some degree is a fact—he seems to have been rather "cared for" than mothered at Pembroke Lodge after the deaths of his parents. It is unlikely that any single substitute mother permanently took him on, more likely a series of caretakers: nurses, nannies, tutors, and other servants, most of whom came and went. Just what these relationships were is all but lost to us, yet we can gauge how strong the attachments were. The nurse and nanny were upper-class household servants whose maternal attachments to the children were often stronger than those of the actual mother. In Russell's case, without a mother, he underwent what Jonathan Gathorne-Hardy calls "multiple mothering" by these people. Gathorne-Hardy emphasizes the power (and often the prudery) of nannies who, in strict nineteenth-century manner, dominated their charges' every action and formed their consciences. Russell's conscience, however, does not seem to have been so exclusively formed, his grandmother having taken a more than usual part in its formation. Nevertheless, the multiple and discontinuous caretaking by nurses and nannies contributed to a state of anxious attachment which made his sexual conscience uneasy in later relations with women. As Gathorne-Hardy points out, the most lasting effect of the nanny on the child was that she left: "They arrived, they stayed a few crucial years, and then they departed."[14] A profound bond was severed and severed again, resulting in the child's rebellious loss of appetite, regression to inappropriate behaviors, and a decreased ability to form and to maintain further attachments. This helps to explain Russell's rebelliousness together with his intensely private inward life of mathematics, immune to such losses.

There is no doubt that up to World War I mathematical creativity served as an escape from human perplexity—creativity of a defensive type. In "The Retreat from Pythagoras," in *My Philosophical Development* (1959), Russell reluctantly admits that mathematics did not bring him the final non-human certainties for which he had wished. To illustrate his earlier hopes, however, he quotes from "The Study of Mathematics" (1907) on mathematics as an art form, a mode of self-transcending beauty in a world of evil and suffering. It is a sort of self-enveloping and self-obliterating exercise: "To reconcile us, by the exhibition of its awful beauty, to the reign of Fate—which is merely the literary personification of these forces—is the task of tragedy. But mathematics takes us still further from what is human, into the region of absolute necessity, to which not only the actual world, but every possible world must conform; and even here it builds a habitation, or rather finds a habitation eternally standing, where our ideals are fully satisfied and our best hopes are not thwarted."[15]

That intermittent attachment was a cause for anxiety plainly shows in his *Autobiography*. Russell mentions several household personages about whom we would be grateful to know more. An example of loss is Miss Hetschel, a nursery governess who left a few days after

Russell's arrival at Pembroke Lodge to be replaced by "a German nurse named Wilhelmina, or Mina for short." The vividness of this recollection is remarkable since Russell was not yet four. His initial protest against Mina taking over (making himself stiff while being bathed) soon gave way to trust and devotion. She taught him German letters; her slaps caused him to cry, but this did not maker her "less of a friend." Significantly Russell writes: "She was with me until I was six years old"—though he does not say what the loss cost him. In the same period there was a nursery maid called Ada who slept in the same room and built the fire each morning. "Freudians may make what they like of this," he comments (I, 27).

But the real issue is the anxiety caused by severed attachments and unpleasant incidents. For example, Russell speaks of the governess who "stormed at me while I endeavoured to learn the multiplication table but was continually impeded by tears," and of the distress caused by a governess telling him that there would be no Christmas presents "unless one believed in Father Christmas," which he did not (I, 32, 35). Of a favorite former governess, Miss Bühler, with whom he could discuss ideas, Russell wrote at age sixteen, that she had briefly returned to Pembroke Lodge but "is gone and I am left again to loneliness and reserve" (I, 52). Verification of the effect of such separation is Frank's perceptive comment in his private Journal for 20 September 1883, five years earlier when Russell was eleven: "I hear the most fearful wailing going on next door, from Bertie and Miss B[ühler] at their approaching separation; there is one of the chief evils of the governess system. Granny and I were agreeing today that she was occasionally very harsh and even unjust with him, and so we are not altogether sorry that she is going" (Russell Archives). It is thus clear how trying Russell found these losses of substitute attachment figures (but about whose temperaments, durations of stay, and at what ages we would have to know in order to say anything more about their shaping of his defenses).

Indeed Pembroke Lodge's interpersonal milieu was changing and complex, but if a hierarchy of female influences is to be suggested—including Russell's aunt Agatha who was only nineteen years older—his grandmother must be placed at the top. It was she who gave continuity of caring in the absence of parents. She "made me love her and gave me that feeling of safety that children need." In a letter of 18 February 1894 to his fiancée, Alys Pearsall Smith, he speaks of being "passionately devoted" to his grandmother. Thus there was anxiety about losing even this source of security: "I remember when I was about four or five years old lying awake thinking how dreadful it would be when my grandmother was dead" (I, 22). He wryly adds that in 1898, after his first marriage, when his grandmother did die "I did not mind at all." Yet he had written to Alys Pearsall Smith on 23 August 1894 that after his grandmother's death he would fear her ghost. More than a ghost was to be feared: his grandmother's austere and moralistic presence was internalized for life.

Making and breaking bonds suggests a pattern of change that later characterized Russell's relational life with women, but I think that intermittent childhood care alone cannot explain it. Loss and substitute caring can, however, help to explain Russell's sensitivity to human suffering at large. A background of depressiveness is necessary for empathy; it allowed Russell to write of "unbearable pity for the suffering of mankind" (I, 13). A fine tragic sense elevates his best writings, a sense refined beyond the youthful negation of this journal passage on nature-induced mourning: "I remember an instant of . . . pain . . . in thinking of the sadness which is always suggested by natural beauty, when the idea flashed across my mind that when most in harmony with Nature I felt most sad, and that therefore the spirit of Nature must be sad and the Universe a mistake."[16] This is one of several aborted attempts to start the mourning process which are identifiable in the early writings. Such healthy symbolic gestures seem to have been insufficient to produce the needed result of reducing sadness and anger to easily tolerated levels. Consequently his reactions divided between the extremes of feeling and inability to feel. On the universal scale, Russell experienced profound pity for suffering, yet he was surprisingly unattuned to the individual suffering caused by his own romantic actions. This discrepancy can be explained by saying that incomplete mourning for early loss allowed identification with suffering in general, but that learned obsessional ego defenses made it possible to inflict suffering (if not positively requiring it) on the lovers whose possessiveness and over-control he feared. Except in the love letters to Lady Ottoline and to Lady Constance, the defensive effect was too strong to reduce the defenses in more than well meant symbolic ways. Even in these deeply moving and truthful correspondences Russell does not see steadily the attraction-repulsion ambivalence as the central dynamic it was. Thus uninterpreted, or inexpertly interpreted, creativity (despite the frequent sharp insights, particularly from Lady Ottoline) leaves the creative person much as he was and may even exacerbate his relational difficulties.

As an intellectual Russell needed mind control over ideas; he had to think through to first principles every idea that interested him. He also needed to control people in his ambit, sometimes subordinating them to his mental activities, but keeping them available to meet romantic and affiliative needs. To account for the situation we should look at the possibility that the obsessional defense—his chronic drive to be creative, together with his Don Juanism—was a function of the relationship with his grandmother during the formative fourteen years of his residence at Pembroke Lodge. Lady John took parental responsibility after a legal complication owing to Russell's free-thinking parents having appointed atheist guardians. On his death-bed Russell's father wrote to his mother, Lady John: "For my two darling boys I hope you would see them much, if possible, and that they might look on you as a mother" (*Autobiography* I, 18). At the death of his grandfather, Lord John, in 1878 (Lord John was twenty-three years older than his wife) Russell was just six. Thereafter Pembroke Lodge was funereal in deference to the great man. Like her acquaintance Queen Victoria, in whose gift the house had been, Lady John took on mourning as a calling. The losses by death which she sustained in her immediate family, losses which also impinged on Russell and permanently saddened the atmosphere of Pembroke Lodge, included: her daughter-in-law Kate, 1874; her grandchild Rachel, 1874; her son John (Lord Amberley), 1876; her husband, Lord John Russell, 1878; her stepdaughter and an infant, Victoria ("Toza"), 1880. Toza's death in childbirth was particularly cruel; it occurred just a week before Russell's eighth birthday. The death left Lady John "fearfully sad and depressed," but still managing, as Frank says in his journal. This was not the end of it; her son Rollo's wife was to die in 1886, and the burden of her daughter Agatha's having "insane delusions" (as Russell later called them) and breaking her engagement, and her son William's commitment to an asylum, could never be completely lifted. Grief and fear of more misfortune pervaded. It is little wonder that Russell should have come to think of religion as based on fear of mystery, defeat, and death, as he says in "Why I Am Not a Christian" (1927). Death had punished his family much more heavily than would be expected even in those days of comparative medical ignorance.

Despite the sadness, Lady John's strong will continued to dominate everyone at Pembroke Lodge, with her daughter Lady Agatha playing a slightly demented celibate role, and her silent but amiable son Rollo following his meteorological and other scientific studies until he left in 1883. Uncle Rollo was too withdrawn to be an effective father substitute, but his drollery and scientific ability were of great value in forming Russell's style and intellectual interests. More needs to be known of this supportive relationship, though Uncle Rollo was later to fall under Russell's condemnation for taking Lady John's part in opposing the first marriage. Russell's grandmother's ambition for him was intense, owing no doubt to disappointment in, and loss of, her children and husband. She had distinct ideas about how social obligation is fulfilled through the proper channels of class and education. Her unworldliness and indifference to money, and a powerful sense of social justice, greatly modified conventionality, but they did not moderate her force of personality.

After Lady John's death, Russell's aunt Agatha appears mainly to have perpetuated her requirements for a virtuous life of service. Lady Agatha was Russell's external voice of conscience, and his relations with her were always ambiguous. As we have seen, she cared for him before he was two when his parents were in Italy, and she must have continued to do so, along with nurses and nannies, after their deaths. Her attempt to teach him the colors and to read ended in frustration, though at age six or seven lessons in constitutional history fared better. She disliked his marriages and affairs, saying so pointedly. Yet in his *Autobiography* Russell is less unkind to his aunt Agatha than he might be, pointing out that for all her old maid eccentricities and repressiveness she had a shrewd wit—as her surviving letters to him show, amidst complaints of loneliness and debility.

From Frank's private journal we find that there were early good relations between the brothers, relations that were to become complicated as time went on. Seven years older, Frank was much away at Winchester and Oxford, but upon return to Pembroke Lodge he was solicitous for and generally kind to his younger brother Bertie. This in any case is how he chose to record the relationship. There were outdoor activities—tree climbing, hide-and-seek and tennis; there were frequent games of skill: draughts and chess. There were even dramatic productions, but most important to Russell was Frank's encouragement to master Euclidean geometry, and in a journal entry for 9 August 1883, Frank records Bertie's remarkable progress in comprehension. Frank's own talent for mathematics, science, and engineering, like Uncle Rollo's, went beyond an aristocrat's amateur level of development. Experimental science and practical engineering were not Russell's forte, but the discovery of prodigious mathematical powers was clearly a delight, and initiated Russell's first major phase of creativity.

Frank rebelled against the Pembroke Lodge ethos whereas, younger and more compliant, Russell let himself be molded by his grandmother's undoubted affection and concern. Disregarding his real gifts, she seems to have thought that she could make of him another liberal prime minister: his adaptation came out looking very much like the obsessional defense. Russell's defensive style was a learned, or at least reinforced, style formed by testing wits with his grandmother. Lady John, an independent-minded Scots Presbyterian (who at age seventy turned Unitarian), had a powerful worldly intelligence, together with a well-formed sense of moral and social duty. As Russell wrote,

> All her ancestry was vehemently Protestant, and she retained something of the outlook of the Covenanters. When I was a boy, she gave me a Bible with her favourite texts written on the fly-leaf. One of these was "Thou shalt not follow a multitude to do evil." She had a rooted conviction that virtue is only to be found in minorities, and this conviction she transmitted to my father. She had a horror of compromise, and viewed all questions that interested her as simple moral issues, in which the good man had only to obey the voice of conscience.[17]

Lady John was widely acquainted with the great literary and political figures of Victorian England. She was a defender of social justice, especially in the cause of Irish Home Rule. She loved intellectual sparring, challenging Russell on literary and political questions and coaching him in the obligations of a liberal reformer. Yet she told him that his free-thinking parents were better off dead, setting about to win him to Christianity and to stimulate his precocity by carefully chosen tutors. He rejected the Christianity, and her wish for leadership ironically manifested itself in his socialism and militant pacifism during World War I. Russell both conformed to his grandmother's wishes and rebelled against them by returning to his parents' atheistic radicalism. He accepted her crusading social awareness but defined it in terms implicitly correcting its distortions. Above all he sensed the danger of bending to her will and moods. He recalls that she related an anecdote which she did not realize disclosed a "morbidness which had produced tragic results in her own children" (*Autobiography* I, 28). He admired her courage in facing family tragedies (she "never lost a certain kind of gaiety") but his criticism is finally devastating: "I do not believe that she ever consciously envied others who had had fewer burdens and more positive happiness, but in the unconscious part of her character she suffered certain strains and distortions which, as time went on, made her increasingly hostile to the claims of vigorous life, with unfortunate results for those who came under her influence" (*Amberley Papers* I, 32).

By this he means specifically that she opposed his father's marriage and felt deep antagonism to his mother, but more is implied. Russell says that Lady John opposed the claims of physical love wherever they emerged: "She loved and respected her husband, but was never physically in love with him. Indeed Puritan inhibitions probably made her incapable of passionate love."[18] His own erotic urgency and inhibition are a function of her attitude through the obsessional defense. Only by ecstasy could he hope to transcend it. Russell does not reconstruct this in full, nor did he realize just how her influence worked on him—to produce not morbidity but chronic drive and sexual anxiety. After losing his parents, Russell suffered at his grandmother's hands another sort of loss, a loss of self-determination through too inclusive and penetrating moral attention.

It was a threat that led to a rebelliousness which filial duty could not mask.

It is not too much to call Russell's grandmother a "pathogenic parent," a loving, doting person too eager for her own children's and for Russell's excellence. She was both repressively dominating and manipulating toward special achievements that had less to do with the actual characteristics of the children than with her own desires. She was a controller, whose impingements might either deepen depressiveness or produce counter control. As a strict Victorian fifty-nine years of age when Russell arrived at Pembroke Lodge, seductiveness toward the boy would be unlikely. Her manipulations were intellectual and took the form of moral cautions. Russell's defenses were correspondingly moral—hypermoral in the sense that the obsessional defense is based on "reaction formation." The reaction formation substitutes high moral principle and purpose for destructive wishes which cannot be consciously entertained. Russell could not afford to be depressed either by capitulating to his grandmother or by admitting how angrily frustrated by her he really was; high moral purpose gave ease. He found that his extraordinary intellectual endowment permitted him at least to fend off his grandmother's incursions. As he grew up his wits sharpened. Her argumentative skills taught Russell that only by argumentation could he rival her. Yet much of what mattered most to him he kept in silence, nurturing an intense inward life.

Despite the loneliness and melancholy of his adolescence, Russell in practice believed in the omnipotence of verbalized thought, in the power of words to encompass and to control all experience. He learned that if only a situation could be verbally formulated, it could be managed by a sort of split-off intellectual functioning. This may have been the basis of his technical interest in language and in logical forms (mainly developed after 1905). But however far he moved into the impersonal study of mathematical logic, the originating relational concern with loss and its effects remained. Precocious mental development carried with it a life-long ambivalence, an attraction to gifted women together with resentment and assertion of intellectual superiority over them.

Russell's substitute mothering appears to have had the sort of stimulating yet threatening effect that is reflected so frequently in the biographies of great men.[19] His remarkable native endowment was coercively shaped by a grandmother suffering from unmet affective needs and caused distorted dependency in the child. Yet her active mind, her keen interest in literature and languages, in the arts and in religion gave unfailing stimulation, as Russell's adolescent journal shows. There is no question that the intellectual companionship was important to them both. All told, he had much to be thankful for in his grandmother. As already noted, he pays her the tribute of saying that "her intense care for my welfare, made me love her and gave me the feeling of safety that children need." At the same time, she insisted on her religious opinions and manipulated him to bring about her moral imperatives. Aunt Agatha, who was exceptionally compliant toward her mother, could be counted on to reinforce them. Russell says that opinions not in conformity with his grandmother's values were treated with "a form of humour, which, though nominally amusing, was really a form of animus." He adds that "I did not at that time know how to reply in kind, and merely felt hurt and miserable" (*Autobiography* I, 46). These feelings became acute in adolescence and, by the time his grandmother tried to block his marriage to Alys Pearsall Smith, they had become verbalized hostile resentment. Her letters of concern for his welfare are in a high degree manipulative, like those of Ernest Pontifex's mother in Samuel Butler's *The Way of All Flesh*:

> You wrote to me once, dear boy, that you dreamed of me constantly by night and thought of me by day and wondered how you could make me happier about you—and I have sometimes thought of putting down on paper what has made me and your Uncle [Rollo] and Aunt [Agatha] so unhappy—in regular order of events and incidents—to help you, even now, to make us happier. Shall I do so? There is nothing I wish more ardently than to have good reason to love dearly the person you marry if I live to see you marry. I am going on pretty well—only a very slow downward progress of the disease. . . . (9 October 1894)

Not only did Granny set up a terrifying barrier against marriage— fear of inherited epilepsy—but she used her ill health to control Russell's loyalty and to make him feel guilty at opposing her will. There is no reason to think that her earlier management of him differed in manner, a manipulative manner bound to produce what the psychiatrist John Bowlby calls "anxious attachment." This anxious attachment to Russell's substitute mother figure carried with it potential anger, resulting from frustrated natural growth. Lady John, who rescued the orphaned Russell from atheist "godparents," could not accept the Quaker blue-stocking Alys, whose emancipated ideas he favored. She had in mind a special destiny for Russell, having him tutored at home perhaps to become another reforming prime minister in the mold of his grandfather. It is true that she enriched his mind with Dante, the English poets, and European novelists, as well as with history, reform politics, and the lore of a great aristocratic family, but at an emotional cost. Having mapped his future, she offered a formidable deterrence to the marriage, the correspondence showing a loyal Bertie trying to out-maneuver her. We infer that in early life he built up an obsessional control system to deal with his grandmother's manipulations, a system which became part of Russell's personality. His obsessional control system became a means of dealing with an active recurring sense that the presence of women must be guarded against to prevent impingement, despite a wish for close relations with them. Conventional morality did not give the freedom to pursue such a strategy.

Much of Russell's creative writing on morality, from *Marriage and Morals* (1929) to "Our Sexual Ethics" (1936) and beyond, attempts to justify an anti-Victorian permissiveness. Like many of the Bloomsbury set, he advocated "creativity" in a love relationship—"spiritual" attachment to a woman—over a feared "possessiveness" by her. But if he thus lent his force to a powerful surge of cultural change, and if he had a profound impact upon the twentieth-century mind, we must also bear in mind the extent to which his creativity was loss-induced and of the obsessional variety.

Notes

1. Bertrand Russell, *Autobiography* I, 43.
2. John Fowles, *Daniel Martin* (Toronto, 1978), p. 285.
3. The typical ambivalent doubleness of attitude toward significant persons in this defense is discussed, for example, by Humberto Nagera in *Obsessional Neuroses: Developmental Psychopathology* (New York, 1976). For obsessional creativity see Anthony Storr, *The Dynamics of Creation* (London, 1972), Chap. 8.
4. In this period Russell's letters show strong interest in Lady Ottoline's analysis with Dr. Vittoz, whose *Treatment of Neurasthenia by Teaching of Brain Control* (London, 1911) he probably read. By 1918 Russell was seriously reading Freud; his qualified acceptance of these theories is well summarized by Alan Wood in *Bertrand Russell: The Passionate Sceptic*, p. 163. Russell's considered judgment on the pretensions of psychoanalysis appears in his satirical "The Psychoanalyst's Nightmare," in *Nightmares of Eminent Persons and Other Stories* (London, 1954).
5. Russell, *Marriage and Morals* (London: George Allen & Unwin 1929), p. 103.
6. Lady Ottoline Morrell to Russell, August 1917. (Unpublished letter, Bertrand Russell Archives, McMaster University.)
7. Ronald W. Clark, *The Life of Bertrand Russell* (London: Jonathan Cape and Weidenfeld & Nicolson 1975), p. 24.
8. Dora Russell, review of Clark, *The Life of Bertrand Russell*, in *The Freethinker* (11 December 1975), p. 189. Dora Russell says much the same in *The Tamarisk Tree*, p. 233.
9. Wood, p. 16. For Russell's version of the story see *Autobiography* I, 31. Bennett and Nancy Simon infer from Amberley's diaries that he was depressed well before the deaths of his wife and daughter. See "The Pacifist Turn: An Episode of Mystic Illumination in Russell's Life," *Russell*, 13 (Spring 1974), 17.
10. See *Autobiography* I, 84–85. The remark on avoidance of deep emotion (p. 86) should be taken in conjunction with this.
11. Wood, p. 16.
12. The effects on personality organization of incomplete mourning are discussed by John Bowlby, "Processes of Mourning," *International Journal of Psycho-Analysis*, XLII (1961), Parts 4-5, 317–40, and "Pathological Mourning and Childhood Mourning," *Journal of the American Psychoanalytic Association*, 11 (1963), 500–41, and in more recent theoretical work.

In *The Philosophers* (Oxford: Blackwell, 1980) Ben-Ami Scharfstein shows the high incidence of early loss of a parent, or parents, among philosophers, shrewdly studying Russell's life in this light.

13. There is more solitary garden object-seeking and communing reported on page 31. A highly developed nature mysticism is evident in the suppressed twenty-second section of the "Greek Exercises" which speaks of his soul communing through its sensitizing by natural objects with the soul of nature. But see also *Autobiography* I, 13.

14. Jonathan Gathorne-Hardy, *The Rise and Fall of the British Nanny* (London: Hodder and Stoughton, 1972), p. 216.

15. Russell, *My Philosophical Development* (London: 1959), p. 211.

16. Russell, "A Locked Diary," *Cambridge Essays 1888–99*, p. 56.

17. Bertrand and Patricia Russell, eds., *The Amberley Papers* (London: Hogarth Press 1937), I, 30.

18. *Amberley Papers* I, 31. Frank's view of his grandmother and of Pembroke Lodge supports, yet in some degree contrasts with, Russell's own. "While the attitude of my father and mother was to face life unashamed and unafraid . . . the Pembroke Lodge attitude was one of halting, of diffidence, of doubts, fears and hesitations, reticences and suppressions, and of a sort of mournful Christian humility. My grandmother Lady John, or as she then was, Countess Russell, was one of the best women who ever lived. She was witty, amusing, kind, even devoted, full of the sense of duty, and of considerable toleration, though rather from loyalty to the tradition of the Whigs than from any inborn conviction that other points of view are really tolerable." See Earl Russell, *My Life and Adventures* (London: Cassell & Co. 1923), p. 33.

19. See Mathew Besdine, "The Jocasta Complex, Mothering and Genius," *Psychoanalytic Review*, 55 (1968), Parts I and II.

3

Reconstructing Meaning: "The Pilgrimage of Life" and Other Early Writings

O how I long to travel back
And tread again that ancient track!
That I might once more reach that plain,
Where first I left my glorious train.
—Henry Vaughan, "The Retreat"

Important factors in Bertrand Russell's contribution to the revolutionary changes in twentieth-century ideas and morals were the sheer volume of his writings, their wide dissemination, and the lucid, easy style he cultivated. Russell was astonishingly productive, writing some 70 books, 2,500 shorter essays and, by estimate, one letter for every 30 hours of his 97-year life. Why was so prolific a writer sometimes unable to complete the books he began? Occasionally he got stuck at writing tasks and could not see them through. The best known instance is his failure to complete the massive epistemological study, *Theory of Knowledge* (1913), abandoned after Ludwig Wittgenstein's severe criticism made Russell feel incapable of doing further fundamental work in philosophy. The other instances are perhaps still more revealing of the tenuousness of his creativity. When a work stirred him to the depths, Russell sometimes found that he could not complete it. Examples are *Prisons*, a philosophy of religion arising from discussions he had in 1911–12 with his lover, Lady Ottoline Morrell, and an autobiography by "Simon Styles" which she thought "too egotistical." In the same period Russell was defeated by his most ambitious literary work, *The Perplexities of John Forstice*. This try at fiction in dialogue form attempts to establish a purpose in life for the too cerebral physicist John Forstice, whose wife has just died. Its contrived dialogue would scarcely have made it a literary success, as Russell's friend, the novelist Joseph Conrad, gently told him. Russell thus abandoned publication plans for this and other powerfully motivated but unsatisfactory literary efforts. To judge these abandoned efforts accurately we should look at his earliest incomplete literary work, *The Pilgrimage of Life*, written in 1902 and probably 1903.

Let us review some childhood circumstances which bear on Russell's sense of personal loss developed in the *Pilgrimage*. His first known experience of loss occurred at eighteen months when his parents left him with grandmother Russell while they sought a better climate for his ailing father. Russell sustained the loss by death of both parents and his sister before he was four. Intimations of legal proceedings over custody may not have escaped even so young a child. Removal from Ravenscroft, his home in Wales, to the austere household at Pembroke Lodge, home of his grandfather, Lord John Russell, who was twenty-three years older than his wife and in declining health, made a seemingly inauspicious beginning to a life.

Russell's remarks in his *Autobiography* often only suggest the importance of what transpired between himself and his substitute caretakers. We would be grateful for much more information about each of the nurses, nannies, and tutors who came and went from Pembroke Lodge. It is clear, however, that a distressing feature of the aristocratic system of paid caretakers for children was that these persons, who sometimes inspired great fondness, were temporary. Like Russell's parents they too were loved and lost, renewing a sense of bereavement which was not given time or occasion to work itself out. A striking feature of the first chapters of Russell's *Autobiography* is his dwelling on the sadness of loss, and on the attachment to his grandmother, about whom his adult feelings were ambivalent. His uncle Rollo and brother Frank were important figures in his childhood too, but the domineering and moralistic personalities of his grandmother and aunt Agatha had more sustained impact. Their wishes for Russell seem to have precluded the active grieving that he needed to clear himself of depressive feelings about his parents and himself. These feelings were in the complicated background of Russell's failing first marriage to Alys Pearsall Smith. When the marriage broke down, Russell experienced another loss—the immediate background of writing *The Pilgrimage of Life*.

The *Pilgrimage* is Russell's first known creative writing. It consists of 21 essay-like meditations or effusions which, although they bear no overall title, evidence shows should be called *The Pilgrimage of Life*.[1] These writings are virtually unknown and first appeared in *Contemplation and Action*, Volume XII of *The Collected Papers of Bertrand Russell*. The sometimes allegorical meditations may seem puzzlingly atypical and perhaps unworthy of inclusion in the canon of a rationalist, but I believe them to be of key importance in understanding Russell the man and thinker. At a certain stage in his development Russell took them very seriously. He notes in his journal for 10 December 1902 that "At Cambridge this time the notion of the Pilgrimage to the Mountain of Truth shaped itself in my mind—an idea in which I hope to find all the expression I want for my religion." This seems to have been a refinement of his earlier conception of the book. He valued seventeenth-century English literature, probably having in mind John Bunyan's *Pilgrim's Progress* and possibly John Donne's "Satire III" (On Religion) and Francis Bacon's "Of Truth." The idea of ascent to truth persisted but by 14 January 1903, when Russell was with his brother-in-law, the connoisseur and art dealer Bernard Berenson, at I Tatti in Florence, the journal shows that he felt dissatisfied with literary progress. "I wrote part of an 'Essay on the Free Man's Worship'; also more of the 'Pilgrimage of Life'; but I was rather uninspired."

Nothing appears to have been done with the *Pilgrimage* until the upsurge of emotion during Russell's affair with Lady Ottoline Morrell reawakened its anguish. On 22 April 1911 he offered to let her see "various unsuccessful attempts at writing, mixed up with private reflections, that I made nine years ago. You will see just how they fail, and why I had to give it up." He says that the only point of Lady Ottoline reading the meditative essays is to "see how they fail," a comment we may doubt in view of their feelings of despair so akin to similar feelings discussed in the letters he was writing her. When he sent Lady Ottoline the *Pilgrimage* papers on 26 April 1911 he commented: "They are a set of disjointed reflections, for the most part, with which I tried to solace myself when I much needed solace." This comment is the key to their meaning. When she reread them on June 1 she thought them "*very* fine, much finer than I admitted to you, or you admitted to yourself." But Russell appears not to have agreed, nor did he reclaim the manuscripts, which were eventually disposed of from Lady Ottoline's estate.

A main difficulty with *The Pilgrimage of Life* is uncertainty about literary form and style. As an apprentice writer Russell was too easily influenced by models not natural to him. The *Pilgrimage's* allegory keeps one eye on Bunyan's *Pilgrim's Progress*, while non-allegorical passages derive from quite other models of evocative, semi-autobiographical writing. Romantic response to nature mingles with the philosopher's wish for precise, unambiguous statement, and mysticism defies the logical urge to define and describe. Some readers will sense Emersonian transcendentalism in these pages, others Wordsworthian nature worship, or even the post-Darwinian raptures of Richard Jefferies' *The Story of My Heart* (1883). But the most likely influence on Russell's design and style was the Belgian mystic and prose rhapsodist Maurice Maeterlinck, whose essay on "The Past" (1901) may well have stimulated Russell's own in the *Pilgrimage*. For a time, as Russell's correspondence shows, Maeterlinck the thinker and stylist impressed him greatly. His brief enigmatic passages, with their seeming profundity, took Russell's fancy before he entirely repudiated Maeterlinck.[2] Similarly attractive must have been Russell's brother-in-law Logan Pearsall Smith's *Trivia* (1903), with its arch and pithy aphorisms hinting at a view of life which is never quite stated. Such efforts to find a language for the soul tempted Russell and, if he failed to make such a language coherent for himself, he certainly revealed the source of anguish leading to the search for form and expression.

Why are the *Pilgrimage* essays incomplete? Purely literary reasons may be suggested, but the reasons advanced here are psychological. It has long been known in psychiatry that grief for loss of persons to whom one is closely attached, and therefore dependent upon for affection and nurture, can lead to depression. Future neurotic depression can be laid in store especially if the loss of parent occurs early in childhood and is too swiftly passed over as alternative caretaking arrangements are made. Freud pointed out such causes of pathological grief reactions in "Mourning and Melancholia" (1917), and since Erich Lindemann's "Symptomatology and Management of Acute Grief" (1944), psychiatric research has looked with increasing interest on the making and traumatic breaking of affectional bonds with consequent adaptive responses. Grief reactions can be normal or disordered, depending on the interpretation of events leading to losses, on allowance for mourning, and on the formation of new affectional bonds. Affective (mood) disorders in mismanaged grief reactions are now an important field for study as shown in the work of John Bowlby.

It is here suggested that Russell's feelings of loss and incomplete mourning, rather than literary reasons, are the main motivations for writing *The Pilgrimage of Life* and for its lack of completion. Russell never succumbed to a major affective disorder, but he was perilously close to it in the period under consideration. He knew that self-control alone could not save him from pain, as he realized and wrote to Mary Murray on 26 September 1903 in an admission of need for therapy of some kind:

> I used to think I could always act rightly by self-control, and so needn't mind what I felt. But that leads to conflict which is horribly tiring, whereas if one can once get the appropriate conditions, one can act rightly with no mental fatigue, or only the unavoidable minimum.

The Pilgrimage of Life belongs to a crisis period that saw Russell's attitude to life change radically as his first marriage crumbled. The year beginning about February 1901 was for Russell one of turmoil, an acute phase of what may be called his "creative illness."[3] The *Autobiography* I, 146, narrates his secular conversion from "flippant cleverness" to the conviction that "the loneliness of the human soul is unendurable" and that only the highest love can penetrate loneliness. The occasion of his transformation had been Evelyn Whitehead's angina attack, witnessed by the Whiteheads' three-year-old boy with whom Russell seems to have identified.[4] It was at about this age that Russell had lost his own parents, a tragedy that left him doubting that the universe is as just as Christianity portrays it. Russell's new sense of each soul's tragic aloneness prompted him to mystical feelings and a sensitivity to beauty; as he says, the habit of "exactness and analysis" subsided. It was just then—late 1901 or early 1902—that relations with Alys completely fell apart, with the marriage continuing in form only. During a bicycle ride, as he tells it, Russell realized that he no longer loved Alys and could not continue to live with her as a wife. The woman he had seen as a saint now seemed malicious; her sincerity seemed insincere, and her once interesting family now filled him with revulsion. The *Autobiography* also reports sexual difficulties with Alys, who told Mrs. Whitehead that Russell could not "bear" children. Alys had a depression whose seriousness is underplayed in his *Autobiography*. But as Russell wrote in a letter to Helen Flexner, "Depression has been the chief thing in Alys's illness, black, utter depression: and at times I have almost envied her part rather than mine."[5] But Russell's sense of her tragic aloneness seems deficient, and it is clear from his 1902–5 journal that he had systematically starved off her need for affection. This was the earliest and most devastating, for the woman, of a series of marital and affectional disruptions that characterized Russell's life. The effect on him of leaving Alys was less one of guilt than of acute separation anxiety, a reawakened fear of being left alone as he had been left alone by the deaths of his parents.

As he says in the *Autobiography*, life at Grantchester, where he and Alys shared a house with the Whiteheads, became lonely and despairing, intensified by the millstream and by the nightingale together with the dawn chorus of other birds haunting his insomnia. "I suffered in a very intense form the loneliness which I perceived a year before to be the essential lot of man." The image of gaunt whitening willows in the wind beckoning from some peaceful land of the dead appears in this autobiographical passage, as it does in two essays included in *The Pilgrimage of Life*. Further, Russell says that he sought comfort in seventeenth-century religious books such as Jeremy Taylor's *Holy Dying*, showing the preoccupation with death which suffuses the essays.

"The Free Man's Worship" is the only writing from this time mentioned in the *Autobiography*, but it is certain that the twenty-one surviving parts of *The Pilgrimage of Life* took their inspiration during this period, though he says in a letter of 26 April 1911 to Lady Ottoline that they were written in a variety of places. He does not mention that "The Free Man's Worship" is closely connected to the suppressed *Pilgrimage* fragments, as may be judged from the allegorical passages in paragraphs 14 and 15 of that famous essay. It is the most fully realized and complete essay in the midst of these meditations and effusions, preserving their essence better than do the companion pieces, "The Study of Mathematics" and "On History." All of this material is closely allied and deserves study as a reparative exercise. The point Russell makes in the *Autobiography* is that as an acute sense of separation and loss swept over him, "the construction of prose rhythms was the only thing in which I found any real consolation."[6]

CHILDHOOD GRIEF

The first essay in *The Pilgrimage of Life* distinguishes between two types of love, that springing from idealizing "admiration" (love of great men of the past and love of God), and that growing from actual personal bonds. Russell notes that "in some mysterious way" the personal attachment of parents and children is internalized; it is "practical" and not chosen by us. By contrast, the "contemplative" love of God springs from admiration and is voluntary. Russell is thinking of the ways that symbols for our basic biological attachment experience are formed. The second brief paragraph to survive in the *Pilgrimage* brings the discussion to the contemplation of childhood events when vulnerability to disrupted attachments is greatest. It introduces the problem of loss, the deepest issue with which Russell had to deal.

Like the two kinds of love, the paragraph on memories of childhood presents a dichotomy. Russell sets Traherne-like rapturous childhood experiences against their transfiguration by Time the Destroyer. He speaks, for instance, of sea, earth, April showers, the golden grass of sunset, and the nightly rustle of poplars lulling him to sleep as impressions to which "doubts and disappointments" had not closed him—a peculiarly negative way of putting it, until we realize that he is trying to bring his readers to feel the sharp disappointment of loss. These transfigured memories have become an idealized realm of good objects: "they glow in a calm, motionless world, bathed in eternal sunshine, and sanctified by regret into the likeness of a dear friend dead." From February 1876 until he went up to Cambridge in 1890, the orphaned Russell had lived with his grandmother at Pembroke Lodge, an aristocratic Victorian house in eleven acres of garden surrounded by Richmond Park. An intensely brooding imagination had taken rise there.[7] The "dear friend dead" prefigures the puzzlement expressed in the sentence of this *Autobiography* passage: "My mother and father were dead, and I used to wonder what sort of people they had been."[8] The connection between their loss, gnawing doubts about life, and idealizing consolation by good objects is established. Russell plainly says that new sorrows induced by loss revive ghosts of past losses, and that with this "wisdom" "joys are turned into pale and ghastly spectres." He does not say that the good objects created in imagination fill the gap of lost parents, but they at least strengthen him to say what the problem really is. It is that of incomplete mourning, of the need for what the psychiatrist Vamik Volkan calls "regrief work," therapy achieved by using "linking objects" to redirect pathological mourning into healthy channels.[9] As noted previously, Russell had cherished such a linking object, a miniature of his dead mother carelessly destroyed by a charwoman to whom his wife Alys had given it for cleaning. Russell's bitterness against Alys for not taking better care of the miniature was devastating, as is clear from a private journal entry dated 14 January 1905. He had been deprived of an almost fetishistic linking object, an object not matched in intensity of feeling until he received a lock of hair from Lady Ottoline Morrell—the lover who replaced Alys. Reminiscent of his feelings toward the destroyed miniature, Russell's words in the *Pilgrimage* establish a link between the mourner and his dead primary attachment object, his mother. Anger at her desertion prevents him naming her directly, but the pathos of separation is clear in the mournful tone and in the high expectation of idealized objects. By such symbolic literary means Russell hoped to complete the mourning which had been left incomplete at the time of his parents' deaths.

To understand Russell's fragile idealization of nature and his pessimism, more needs to be said about pathological mourning. In *Loss, Sadness and Depression* John Bowlby deals with the disordered variants of the mourning which is a normal and necessary process whenever there is loss of attachment figures. Russell's literary myth of the human condition as primarily tragic and uncertain may be seen as an expression of loss and disordered mourning. For instance, in *The Perplexities of John Forstice* (1912) he insists on "the fundamental pain of the universe," a conviction that man's place in the cosmic order is insignificant and that suffering follows from our smallness and vulnerability. So acute a sense of mortality, and of cosmic indifference to it, probably stems more from Russell's incomplete grieving for his lost parents—and secondarily, his sister—than it does from any special knowledge of the universe. That he was too quick to see the entire human condition as tragic does not mean that he failed to make heroic efforts to assert the nobility of mind and spirit. Russell's writings in this period certainly assert human dignity in the face of the possibility of an uncaring universe. But his wish to reconstruct the facts of his tragic personal situation was more than he could manage alone. *The Pilgrimage of Life* is autobiographical allegory set at a safe distance from the actuality of Russell's disrupted early attachments. (Not until the *Amberley Papers* [1937] and the *Autobiography*, begun in 1931, did he consider directly the facts and feelings of loss.) Some further observations on attachment psychology will indicate why the *Pilgrimage* is only a set of well-intentioned fragments.

Bowlby writes that disordered mourning goes on without the mourner's full awareness, yet it powerfully shapes his attitudes and relationships. Despite a "prolonged absence of conscious grieving," he is motivated by a wish to grieve for his loss and may become physically or emotionally ill because he cannot do so.[10] Psychotherapy for a wide variety of complaints may reveal encapsulated grieving for loss. The urge to search for a lost attachment object is present (to paraphrase Bowlby) with anger and/or self-reproach readily aroused, but sorrow and sadness absent. Life expectations are thus organized on a false basis, or they fall into disarray. To Bowlby's analysis may be added a reparative urge present in some bereaved and depressed people who have creative talent. In Russell's instance his massive gifts were bent toward constructing a reparative myth in the *Pilgrimage*, and in other such writings of the decade following, but he could not let himself feel the full force of loss and of the wish to mourn. Writing an allegory seemed a perfect strategy to move closer to true feelings without being overwhelmed by them. As letters show from both the period of his courtship and marriage to Alys Pearsall Smith and in his affair with Lady Ottoline Morrell, Russell feared and was subject to depressions. Judging by his letters to Lady Ottoline, as his relationships became more irregular the threat of depression increased. Suicide was sometimes on his mind. Fear of lack of sustaining attachment drove him to accept the aesthetic consolations she taught him. As Bowlby says, ego defenses try to exclude unwanted information of depressive sadness. Writing may indeed be mainly defensive, but Russell did not become a heavily defended aesthete. His attempts at creative writing sought to portion out sadness in acceptable amounts and to put it in a framework of understanding, even if this was only to be a literary rather than a cosmic framework. The urge was healthy—toward ego repair and restructuring pessimistic feelings about the world. How successful was the result?

THE NEED TO MOURN MISSED

Russell's *Pilgrimage* essays successfully convey melancholy and despair but they leave an enigma. The reader does not understand without additional biographical evidence why Russell should be so despairing. The allegorical mode he adopted did not permit him to open the enigma of melancholy, to break through to the relational issues causing it. These we gather from chance remarks in the *Autobiography* such as that when he was happiest in love with Alys, feeling the purest joy, "it seems to transcend itself and fall suddenly to haunting terrors of loss. . . ."[11] This he links with "the gradual discovery, one by one, of the tragedies, hopeless and unalleviated, which have made up the lives of most of my family . . ."—referring to other family deaths than the tragic illnesses and deaths of his own parents. The *Pilgrimage* essays appear to be the first distillation of this melancholic realization, Russell's assent to Keats's proposition that the world is a "vale of soulmaking." In the third *Pilgrimage* paper he sets up a dichotomy between pure soul and the world which takes it captive in marriage.

In the years of bondage the memory of freedom fades away, regrets

become rarer, the iron enters into the soul, and the image of un-
trammelled joys grows pale.

A malign reflection on marriage is evident, but children of the
marriage may ease its discomfort, he says. The essay's closing hope of
comfort is not very convincing.

Writing further of the comforters of the soul (Courage, Love, and
Peace), Russell expands on compensations, but without saying why
they are needed. Nowhere does he give reasons for his search for
spiritual reassurance or for rationalizations in other of the essays of
gentle death as desirable. Creation and destruction lie close together,
with Russell recreating the life-supporting synthesis he feared had
been destroyed. Insistence on pain, suffering, pity, and the soul's
comforters make little sense without realizing the developmental
damage from which Russell had suffered by parent loss and by the
inadequate replacement provided by his grandmother and her household at Pembroke Lodge. Much of what Stephen Kern calls the
"explosive intimacy" of the Victorian family was true of this one.
Russell felt both stimulated and entrapped in his grandmother's
network of resident family and retainers; she dominated his life
through changes of nurses, nannies, and tutors whose kind attentions
Russell craved. If they were transient, his grandmother and Aunt
Agatha were ever present, together with silent Uncle Rollo.[12] Intimacy with these living persons could not compensate for the mother
and father he had lost. Talk of the protective cloister, of friendship,
and of a lost comfort in religion at least make sense in "On Comforters
of the Soul" when Russell writes:

> In the love of the dead, when the impatience of impotent rebellion has
> died away, contemplation can still find a sober joy; they too were in this
> world, they too are forever a part of the strange fabric of existence.

Here recreation by words begins to reverse his despairing sense of
destruction. He goes on to speak of "the mysterious bond of motherhood, consecrated in its very beginning by pain and the shadow of
death." Motherhood "creates a tie which is deeper, more lasting,
more profound than any that men can know." The family may
sometimes be a Moloch but it is the basis of our social relations and

gives a sense of continuity through time. Clearly a reconstructive effort is under way, and it extends to Russell's view of nature:

> Every hedgrow, every primrose, every winter robin, has the strange aroma of sadness, the mystical magic, that lives like a wraith in scenes of the past; where the deep intimacy of childhood, the thought of smiles that are gone and of voices we shall hear no more, hallows the earth. . . .

This is a spontaneous symbolic attempt to carry through the mourning of childhood which, all the evidence indicates, Russell did not complete. He was certainly aware of the ravages of death, complaining in his *Autobiography* of "the perpetual gloom which hangs like a fate over P[embroke] L[odge]."[13] This was the gloom of mummification, not of true mourning. It was less therapeutic than cultic and self-pitying. Like Queen Victoria's morbid mummification of the memory of her husband, Prince Albert, Russell's grandmother had enshrined the memory of her husband, Lord John Russell, the former prime minister, a statesman much respected and honored by the Queen. Lord John died when Russell was just six (a fact he repeats in *Autobiography* I, 20, 32). Russell does not admit to being touched by the old man's passing, perhaps because it had led to the mournfulness he so disliked at Pembroke Lodge. While the great man's memory was venerated by Lady John, Russell's aunt Agatha, and others of the household, that of his parents was not. We may be sure that all of the elaborate Victorian funeral and mourning customs had been observed in Lord John's honor. Yet for Russell's free-thinking parents these had been scanted. Russell's grandmother told him that his parents were better off dead, and their place of burial at Ravenscroft in Wales had become a matter of contention.[14] Russell says nothing in his *Autobiography* of a formal period of mourning customary for Victorian children who had lost parents. Through the nineteenth century mourning etiquette for children had relaxed, so that by the 1880s a contemporary report notes: "It is desirable that children should be put into mourning dress as seldom as possible; only in fact for the very nearest relatives. The little children do not understand it and it is absurd to invest them with signs of grief they cannot feel. Absence of a positive colour is quite sufficient mourning for children."[15] Yet from

1874 to 1876, when Russell's parents and his sister Rachel died, such customs would have been partially observed, if not in every ritualistic detail. Russell makes no mention of these all-important rites of passage expected in the aristocracy to which he belonged. Artificial and devoid of true feeling though Victorian mourning could sometimes be, its neglect indicates a serious psychological oversight on the part of Russell's caretakers. As James Stevens Curl writes: "Mourning was obligatory in Victorian times, and if the customs were not complied with, it was reckoned to be a sign of disrespect or worse."[16] It seems likely that Russell's grandmother's lack of thorough-going mourning for her son and daughter-in-law, mourning in which Russell and his brother Frank could have participated fully, betokened disapproval. It is true that Lady John's loss of six family members in six years was unusually cruel and that she was chronically unwell; nevertheless it seems right to say that her moral disapproval of Russell's father's and mother's free-thought prevented the easing of grief which formal, sincerely felt mourning would have given the orphaned Russell. Although he was not yet four when these events took place, evidence indicates that true mourning at this age is possible. While such very young children seldom react to parent loss by weeping, they do yearn, a precondition for healthy mourning. As Bowlby writes:

> When adults are observant and sympathetic and other conditions are favourable, children barely four years old are found to yearn for a lost parent, to hope and at times to believe that he (or she) may yet return, and to feel sad and angry when it becomes clear that he will never do so.[17]

But conditions were not favorable, and it was probably assumed that Russell would simply "forget" his dead parents. Thus the matter was prematurely closed, and an atmosphere promoting later healthy accommodation was not established. His grief became encapsulated, seeking lonely symbolic outlets, especialy when later sustaining attachments were threatened or broken. He was forced to acquiesce in the circumstances, but acquiescence is not full acceptance of loss that healthy mourning can bring. In "The Essence of Religion" (1912), all that Russell salvaged from the unfinished *Prisons*, he wrote:

> Acquiescence in private griefs is an essential element in the growth of universal love and the impartial will.
>
> Acquiescence does not consist in judging that things are not bad when in fact they are so. It consists in freedom from anger and indignation and preoccupied regret. Anger and indignation against those who cause our griefs will not be felt if universal love is strong; preoccupied regret will be avoided where the desire of contemplative freedom exists.[18]

These noble but too matter-of-fact words signal a compromise that he had not wished to perpetuate in 1902.

Trying to balance despair with hope, he closed "On the Comforters of the Soul" with an observation on our collective fate, which is really a recognition of his own.

> We are all orphans and exiles, lost children wandering in the night, with hopes, ideals, aspirations that must not be choked by a heartless world. If some grow too soon weary and faint-hearted, it is for those whose courage is strong to give brave words, to keep alive the dreams of the Golden City.

In Bunyan's *Pilgrim's Progress* Christian triumphantly completes his dangerous trek to the resplendent Celestial City of God. Secular Russell, however, has nothing like Bunyan's assurance of safe harbor. The essays continue on a lesser trackway, holding out reduced hopes but speaking more plainly of the losses and inner weaknesses likely to prompt such literary reconstructions. Russell writes of Truth in "The Worship of Truth" as "a stern and pitiless God" who may "blast the lives of those we love"; yet we must serve Truth because only by doing so are the shining lights "kindled on the mountain-tops by which, far off in the plain, humanity is guided in the night of fear and perplexity." Russell's attempt to revive for his time the seventeenth-century idea of death as a world of light (as found for instance in Henry Vaughan's poem "They are all gone into the world of light," a poem he commended to Lady Ottoline on 3 January 1912) does not succeed. The Christian belief system in which he was raised could no longer sustain such a supposition in the post-Darwinian age. In this way the *Pilgrimage* marks the collapse of a metaphysic which Russell belabored in "Why I Am Not a Christian" (1927), and indicates why he came to see logic and mathematics as more purely contemplative activities than mere supplications of Christian prayer.

Similarly with the Romantic appeal to nature in *The Pilgrimage of Life* we feel the end of a tradition rather than its renewal. "The Message of Nature," only three sentences long, tries to establish "a voice speaking straight to experience and sorrow"; but Russell cannot summon the words to make us believe, as Wordsworth and Keats do, that "beauty is eternal." A related paragraph renews the attempt to gain conviction that "beyond the life of man, the untroubled world of sea and stars and sun endures, a reproach, and yet a balm, to the wounded spirit stricken by the terror of its own brief torture." This rhetorical invention of the suffering soul is too strong for the remedy it seeks. The troubling human condition takes precedence over any sovereign remedies for separation and loss that might be left over from Romanticism's assumption of the spiritual in Nature. Only Russell's favorite image of "willows whitened by the passing wind" arrests the reader's attention. But it too is sentimental, lacking the resonance of natural images found, for instance, in the early books of *The Prelude* where Wordsworth speaks of his own sorrowful experience of loss, grieving, and symbolic repair. "Willows whitened by the passing wind" reappears in "The Ocean of Life" (June, 1902), and can be traced to actual trees seen on sad walks in the fields near Grantchester during the separation from Alys, but somehow "the secret message of nature" does not take us deep enough into human nature to make the difference between literature and the wishful thinking of a depressive seeking new attachment objects.[19]

Much of what Russell wrote in the *Pilgrimage* seems tense, moralistic, and incompletely realized as art. Neo-Bunyanesque allegory is misplaced. An untitled allegory about a youth whose soul descends to earth addresses the parent-centered despair from which transcendent love offers rescue. In this piece Russell speaks indirectly of mourning, touching on his separation from Alys: "she whom you loved is among the mourners, and you stabbed the young hope at whose tomb-stone she is offering flowers." The youth learns pity and temporarily becomes a saint, only to face death and despair once more in an unregenerative cycle: "and alone again, as he had begun, he ended the life he had not dared to live." This shows that re-grief work, late mourning by using real or implied symbolic objects, is not progressing. The mourning in the shady garden of delights for which Russell calls in the previous piece, "The Two Races of Man," also seems left in doubt. He pictures both desert and restorative garden, with many pilgrims in the parched desert never gaining solace from the "fountain of joy." Their tears may water the garden but they do not attain its protection, though Death takes many to fulfilment there. The vision ends on a negative note with some pilgrims simply falling asleep near their loved ones outside the garden. The piece lacks the sharpness and clarity of meaning which allegory traditionally promotes by stimulating imagination to work pictorially on abstract religious ideas. Russell was too far removed from his prototypes in Spenser and Bunyan for allegory to work.

Perhaps the best among these essays is "The Past," a poignant statement of sadness, an elegy for a lost "calm and smiling land, bathed in eternal sunshine, from which life's voyage has separated us by a whole sea of sorrow, renunciation and loss." He writes with less manneredness than in earlier pieces about a lost enchanted country which only words can conjure back. But here too the conclusion is negative: he is troubled by unwanted depressive information, a product of unmourned loss. "And at length the Past so invades the inmost recesses of feeling that happiness, even in the very moment of its being, seems already gone, and present joys bring with them their own wraiths as uninvited guests." The thought seems continued in a further paragraph about how hopes die and are received by "the kingdom of the Past." Now the wraiths are "spectres" who haunt the conscious world, as Russell speaks of necessary avoidances if dangerous memories are not to "imprison us in the dungeon of despair, lest, for a moment of terror, we live once more the life of pain." He fears "the sharp stab of loss" and dares not look to "that beautiful country of the Past" containing lost loves, friendships, and joys. Sadness and active mourning are evident, even as he speaks of resisting them; but we do not know how far the impulse to mourn carried him.

It is interesting to note, however, that in "The Free Man's Worship" he reversed this view of the past, giving it "magical power"—cessation of change and striving. It is a realm of peace. The past becomes a still world of eternal values, more Platonic than specter-haunted. "Its beauty, to a soul not worthy of it, is unendurable; but to a soul which has conquered Fate it is the key to religion." We do not know just when these words were written, but they suggest that Russell at least realized the need to challenge fate by a full course of mourning his losses. There is still further evidence of attempts to mend the fractured past, or at least to reorder its broken pattern. In the closing paragraphs of "On History," written in March 1903, Russell speaks of the past, as opposed to the present, being "truly real." "Only the dead exist fully, the lives of the living are fragmentary, doubtful, and subject to change; but the lives of the dead are complete, free from the sway of Time." The prose is of the same meditative sort as in the *Pilgrimage*, but it is firmer, suggesting an attempt to confront the problem of loss and that Russell was taking comfort in thoughts of a sort of secular heaven, a Valhalla, where all losses are safely enshrined. Perhaps this is not the mourning process itself, but it is not evasion either. Russell was making correct associations to his past in the service of the health he perceived and wanted.

Moral Teachings

The remaining *Pilgrimage* essays tend to exhort to moral virtue rather than to probe deeper into the substrate of loss-caused depressiveness. They are spiritual directives, self-teaching exercises, rather than continuing analyses of Russell's own condition. These he had perhaps taken as far as it was safe to do in that crisis of his creative illness. In 1902–3 no psychodynamic theory was available to steady him in the absence of religion. When the romantic notion that creative writing alone could be therapeutic lost its impetus, there was little left for Russell but to turn to the moralism of his youth. Moderated by a wish for literary excellence, the moral impulse (the last vestige of his grandmother's decayed protestantism) took over to conclude the *Pilgrimage* in what seems the only way it could be concluded. The tone of the closing essays is not consistent, ranging from mellow appeals for love to all who suffer (in an essay on old age bringing wisdom) to Carlyle-like exhortation to become heroes in "The Communion of Saints." Themes and concerns begin to show predictable Victorian and Edwardian moralism.

There are, however, some formulations of Russell's inner situation to be noticed in these meditations. "The Return to the Cave" is a Platonic allegory of inward search, of the soul's withdrawal and return in an improved condition. "In the darkness of the cave, we must remember the golden world above; for only so can we keep before us the distant goal of all the weariness and the labour." He has not closed the gap between an idealized golden world and harsh feelings of loss and emptiness in this world. Russell recommends austerity to control emotion, even the emotion of human affection, with resulting drastic reduction of affect for which "a substitute may be found which outweighs the loss." By "substitute" he means not only uplifting moral action but "the community in sorrow and devotion" to which the seeker may turn. But a resumption of attempts to mourn does not seem in view. This is the language of primary attachment loss and defensive renunciation of affect. Russell does not say that "renunciation of private desires" may be a false solution to the exile's quest. Nor does he say what the compensations of emotional austerity may be, trying instead to convince his readers that the individualistic "cult of the dignity of Man" fostered by Carlyle, Ibsen, and Nietzsche is wrong. Their views too easily lead to anarchy, cruelty, and oppression. Man is a social being, Russell says, but the feeling given by the essay is that indeed the journey is painful and entirely individual. ("Each human being is born single, separate, enclosed as in a dungeon by strong walls of egotism," as he says in "Austerity," the true emphasis of these meditations.) Russell shows himself to be fully as much in need of an individual solution to his anguish as Carlyle, Ibsen, or Nietzsche. The last paragraph of "The Return to the Cave" places him exactly in this anguished modern tradition of the soul seeking its quietus, but the specific task of mourning is bypassed. Had Russell been able to write the *Pilgrimage* with the same candor as that of his closing evocation of moments at Grantchester, the book would have been more worthy of the tradition to which it aspires and, psychologically, a stronger aid to mourning.

> Oh Nature is great, and strong, and calm. All night I tossed, fretted and fevered by the little problems of my petty life. At last the nightingale ceased, the birds of day began to salute the light, and I looked out upon the dawn—exquisite, still, serene, the same now as in all the

ages of man's sorrow. Little clouds drifted slowly across the sky, and the morning star shone through them. The unruffled water reflected the trees and the mill, and over the meadows lay a quiet mist, white and beautiful in the first light of morning. Not all that is external to man is hostile—from age to age that beauty has endured and will endure, a soothing Balm, and yet a tonic, to the wounded soul crushed by the terror of its own brief torture.

The passage ends hoping for the compensation which in fact is evidenced in the essays following it, "Gentleness" and "The Forgiveness of Sins." But like "The Return to the Cave" awareness of torture and death is so deeply embedded that compensations remain in doubt. For Russell the subject of loss was compulsive; he could not gain much distance from it. It is little wonder then that the *Pilgrimage*'s concluding two essays should be religious, asking what form of religious truth there remains to grasp.

Russell seems almost set for a conversion narrative such as John Bunyan's seventeenth-century *Grace Abounding to the Chief of Sinners*. But the historic moment had passed and the heavy qualifications on Christian faith placed by such latter-day pilgrims as Thomas Carlyle, Mark Rutherford, and Edmund Gosse left Russell unsupported. So in "The Atonement," a would-be grammar of assent, Russell finds himself unable to accept Christian hope on the grounds that God permits the good and the just to suffer while the wicked prosper. He settles for secular individualistic self-purification, all that could be salvaged from the rigors of his grandmother's Presbyterian, and later Unitarian, faith. Renunciation of pleasure, stoical acceptance of pain, and stern self-rule without expectation of easy reward are his teachings. The result will be purification of soul, proof against "fears and terrors," and a readiness for death, "a kind and faithful friend, a beneficent healer of all wounds." The essay in the *Pilgrimage* called "Religion" is not a profound analysis of the meaning of mysticism or religious experience as Christianity teaches it, but a secular advocacy of "virtue" and "excellence." A "heroic human life is the best, the only truly good thing" we have to assert against fate and the reign of matter, he wrote. There is little to show that Russell had found a trustworthy road back from despair in the absence of some kind of therapeutically induced mourning.

"Religion" affirms too broadly what Russell affirms with due qualification (given his growing sense of the tragic) in "The Free Man's Worship." There he wisely refrains from implying that a moral transformation is at hand, saying only that man is "to expel all eagerness of temporary desire, to burn with passion for eternal things," and to give sympathetic encouragement to the "divine fire" when it is kindled in other hearts. Thus man becomes free by seeing clearly the predicament of his littleness in an uncaring universe. He must grapple with the thought of being "condemned to-day to lose his dearest, to-morrow himself to pass through the gate of darkness."[20] By facing up to mutability and loss, by being open-eyed rather than trust in the hope of an afterlife impossible to demonstrate, Russell surely began to overcome his own anguish. He was building up the courage to face "what is" rather than fabricate hopes beyond any possibility of realization. He was developing the tragic view of life to take fully into account, but without yielding to it, the unavoidable depressiveness of much human experience. Perhaps Russell's greatest discovery in this period was the tragic sense of life, that sadness inhering at the core of things. In "The Free Man's Worship" he writes, "Of all the arts, Tragedy is the proudest, the most triumphant; for it builds its shining citadel in the very centre of the enemy's country."[21] Whatever is created and lives is liable to wasteful dissolution and loss. His own writing heightened the sense of life being fragile and transient; and he began to measure the actual sadness of his own losses. Unable to pursue mourning to its natural conclusion, he at least found consolation in the tragic sense of life. Ancient Greek literature was a potent stimulus, along with his "conversion" of early 1901, teaching him that "the loneliness of the human soul is unendurable" and that the highest love must penetrate it. Gilbert Murray's reading from his translation of Euripides' *Hippolytus* profoundly stirred Russell "by the beauty of the poetry." In a letter to Murray after reading the play Russell says:

> Your tragedy fulfils perfectly—so it seems to me—the purpose of bringing out whatever is noble and beautiful in sorrow; and to those of us who are without a religion, this is the only consolation of which the spectacle of the world cannot deprive us.[22]

The Tragic Sense of Life

It is against the aesthetic background of seeing portrayed the decline and loss of persons of great promise that we must place Russell's literary efforts to mourn. His deepening sense of the tragic helped him to assimilate "the gradual discovery, one by one, of the tragedies, hopeless and unalleviated, which have made up the lives of most of my family."[23] "Hopeless and unalleviated" is not an acceptable state of affairs, and to make sense of it is a task to which literary creativity of a higher order than Russell's at this time would have been necessary. Only in his confessional letters to Lady Ottoline did he find a medium ample to the task. But his massive anguish was often too great even for the brilliant therapeutic dialogue that began in 1911 and continued in some form until her death in 1939. As he confessed in a letter of 24 June 1914: "I have a very intense and terrible spiritual loneliness."

As Russell told Lady Ottoline, he had written the *Pilgrimage* "to solace myself." He did not and could not fully explain the gravity and extent of his need to mourn. Thus an essential phase of his "creative illness" was left incomplete, and he remained a moralist rather than becoming another Freud or Jung specializing in the ways of the unconscious. Grief was an immeasurable feature of his life and one we cannot judge except to estimate its magnitude from recent work by John Bowlby and others on the process of mourning. It is suggested that Russell needed to reconstruct his assumptive world and to redirect attachment after the disruption caused by ceasing to love Alys. Seven or eight years of marriage had increasingly unsettled the precarious psychological organization caused by early parent loss and intermittent caretaking through childhood. As noted, he suffered from broken attachments to nurses and nannies, and from ambivalent reactions to his grandmother. Nearly overmastered by powerful women in his childhood, Russell developed an obsessional defensiveness which permanently complicated the very constancy with women as lovers that would have helped to quiet the fear of loss. As it was, he brought about more losses in his relational life, confirming the fear of mutability. But he must have seen his course of acting as producing the lesser of two evils.

The Pilgrimage of Life is artificial and contrived because the material is too painful to relax about while writing it. Russell had uncovered massive sadness, longing and rage—the sadness of incomplete mourning, longing for lost parents and later caring persons, together with rage against the universe for letting such things happen. Until "The Free Man's Worship," with its cosmic cry of pain, he found no adequate reparative literary form by which to deal with all he felt. "The Free Man's Worship" gains powerful literary authority because the form invented itself out of the essay tradition rather than being an unsteady attempt at blending allegory with Maeterlinck. Both features are there, but without the self-conscious constraint. The reason for the more freeing consequences of "The Free Man's Worship" seems to be that the essay deals mainly with rage against the universe rather than examining the sadness and longing with which Russell could not get on in The Pilgrimage of Life. His subject at last is manageable, but the self-diagnostic and self-reconstructive efforts were therefore correspondingly limited. Soundings of the self are replaced by a finished metaphysical statement, beautiful in its aesthetic wholeness but without the penetration to reach and to initiate resolution of the basic conflict from which Russell suffered.

The Pilgrimage's meditations and allegories are heavy with the sense of trying to carry a burden too great for them. The masterpieces of meditation, such as Pascal's Pensées, are both startlingly allusive and crisp in their brevity; in a few words they evoke mystery and the personal predicament of living in a universe which does not answer our questions. The best allegory, as in Bunyan's Pilgrim's Progress, is childlike, almost frivolous in its story-book simplicity, while stirring the profoundest associations to depressive risk, death, and judgment. This disjunction is alive with the promise of aesthetic resolution in the mind. Great narrative poetry, such as Wordsworth's Prelude, can handle separation and sorrow in the associative flow of life events set into healing nature. The successful writer must gauge his own depression against the vehicle chosen to contain and reconcile it. Russell's incomplete grief-work seems to have been at the very base of his personality organization. How was he to master that task without the literary gifts of a Pascal, a Bunyan, or a Wordsworth? Russell's imagination was divided between its extraordinary capacity for mathematical abstraction and a compelled attention to the facts of existence as they were. His moralism is invariably down to earth and circumstantial. Imaginative fiction of any sort did not come naturally to him, nor did poetry. *The Pilgrimage of Life* is therefore a false start but in the right direction, had he seen what it was trying to communicate to him about the need actually to mourn his losses. In the *Pilgrimage* he simply recreated the funereal and mummified atmosphere of his childhood at Pembroke Lodge without getting to the specific issues of who had died and what he felt about the losses.

The Pilgrimage may seem an embarrassment which Russell's admirers have difficulty explaining. It seems entirely out of character and impossible to reconcile with his high-spirited rational skepticism. It would be tidier if these writings were disqualified in any critical assessment of Russell the thinker. On the contrary, the *Pilgrimage* is core material for understanding all of Russell. It portrays the man as he essentially was, his extraordinary intellect fuelled by griefs and obsessive conflicts for which, painfully often, he could find neither word nor symbol. There is a certain truth in associating "The Study of Mathematics" with "On History" and "The Free Man's Worship" in that it praises the refuge from conflict given by mathematics—a too ready refuge perhaps preventing him from working still harder to find courage to speak less brokenly the language of loss-caused depressiveness. When he began his *Autobiography* in the 1930s, the pressure of motivating anguish had subsided, and his reconstruction was altogether cooler than it deserved to be. Russell's purely literary efforts in the 1901–3 period of creative illness do not indicate what a new line of discovery might have been. As it turned out, the personal letter of his vast private correspondence was to be his medium of genius, about which much more needs to be said. But *The Pilgrimage of Life* itself tells us what titanic forces underlay Russell's creative efforts as a writer. It directs us both backward and forward in time—backward to a crisis when unalloyed rationalism ceased to be the sole criterion for action, and forward to the many years of crusading as a popular moralist on the topics of love and war.

Notes

1. The meditative essays are ordered according to the page numbers and occasional dates Russell gave them, but the series is discontinuous, indicating gaps where material was lost or never written. There is bound to be conjecture in any ordering of this material. *The Pilgrimage of Life* appears in Volume 12 of *The Collected Papers of Bertrand Russell*, pp. 31–55.

2. Bertrand Russell, *Autobiography* I, 151. Letters to Helen Flexner of June 27 and August 2, 1902, show Russell to be enthusiastic about Maeterlinck's *Le Temple Enseveli* where he makes "the Past a product of ourselves, which we can alter and beautify as we will." But by September 16 he told her that he had changed his mind about Maeterlinck.

3. The "creative illness" discussed by Henri F. Ellenberger in *The Discovery of the Unconscious* (London: Penguin, 1970), is also discussed by Sir George Pickering in *Creative Malady* (London: Allen & Unwin, 1974).

4. Bennett and Nancy Simon, "The Pacifist Turn," pp. 18–19.

5. Russell to Helen Flexner, 11 November 1902.

6. *Autobiography* I, 149–50.

7. *Autobiography*. When Russell's aunt Agatha gave up Pembroke Lodge in 1902 his melancholic feeling about it was heightened. As he wrote to Helen Flexner (14 October 1902): "I paid a last visit there, and it was inexpressibly sad to see the last of the old garden which I have loved almost more than if it had been a human being, to think of profane hands making it new and smart, destroying the beautiful memories of the Past which live in every part of it, and thinking nothing of all the joys and sorrows which seemed inalienable property."

8. Ibid., I, 20.

9. Vamik D. Volkan, *Primitive Internalized Object Relations* (New York: International Universities Press, 1976), p. 219. See also "The Linking Objects of Pathological Mourners", *Archives of General Psychiatry*, 27 (1972).

10. John Bowlby, *Loss: Sadness and Depression* (London: Hogarth, 1980), p. 138.

11. *Autobiography* I, 85.

12. Stephen Kern, "Explosive Intimacy: Psychodynamics of the Victorian Family" in *The New Psychohistory* (New York: Psychohistory Press, 1975).

13. Ibid., I, 85.

14. Ibid., I, 31.

15. Quoted by John Morley, *Death, Heaven and the Victorians* (London: Studio Vista, 1971), p. 72.
16. James Stevens Curl, *The Victorian Celebration of Death* (London: David and Charles, 1972), p. 9.
17. Bowlby, *Loss: Sadness and Depression*, p. 285.
18. Russell, *The Basic Writings*, ed. R. E. Egner and L. E. Dennon (New York: Simon and Schuster, 1961), p. 572. In "The Free Man's Worship" Russell speaks of wisdom coming of learning "resignation" and "renunciation" of our wishes.
19. *Autobiography* I, 149–50.
20. "The Free Man's Worship" in *Mysticism and Logic*, p. 59.
21. Ibid., p. 56.
22. *Autobiography* I, 156. Russell went on to confide in Murray, writing just before the period of composing *The Pilgrimage of Life*: "I have been making myself a shrine, during the last eight months, where I worship the things of beauty that I have known; and I have learnt to live in this worship even when I am outwardly occupied with things that formerly would have been unendurable to me." (December 16, 1902)
23. *Autobiography* I, 85.

4

A Pathway Found: Russell's Conversion of 1901

Mystic conversion is a single and abrupt experience, sharply
marked off from the long, dim struggles which precede and
succeed it.

—Evelyn Underhill, *Mysticism*

THE BACKGROUND OF PACIFISM

When nuclear weapons were used in 1945, it became apparent that
mankind one day might destroy itself through warfare of unprece-
dented terror. Bertrand Russell was among the first to insist that the
bombings of Hiroshima and Nagasaki announced a world entirely
different from any previously known and that a new geopolitics would
have to be devised to sustain life on earth. The Russell–Einstein
Manifesto (1955) states that the dangers of nuclear weaponry far
exceed the ideological split of capitalist from communist which gave
rise to the Cold War. The preservation of any ideology could not
justify the levels of destruction predictable in a nuclear war. Russell's
magnificent essay, "Man's Peril" (1954), contains the words: "I
appeal, as a human being to human beings: remember your humanity, and forget the rest. If you can do so, the way lies open to a new
Paradise; if you cannot, nothing lies before you but universal death".[1]
He had moved far from the mathematical logician of the turn of the
century. Russell the philosopher-statesman came onto the world scene
with a clear message about human survival: "If mankind survives, my
work on behalf of [nuclear disarmament] will be the most important
thing I have done. What is the truth on logic does not matter two pins
if there is not one alive to know it."[2]

Simple though it may seem, Russell's concern with the survival of mankind has a complex history. His view of war changed with circumstances. During the First World War Russell was a powerful advocate of conscientious objection, and he spent time in prison for his anti-war views. The courage of his pacifism was perhaps greatest then. The Second World War found him reluctantly convinced that the Nazi tyranny had to be resisted by armed force, though he saw in Stalin a menace as great as Hitler. In an uncharacteristic moment in 1948, Russell suggested war against Russia to prevent her becoming a nuclear power. To those who objected that he was being inconsistent with his pacifist principles, Russell replied, "I believe that some wars, a very few, are justified, even necessary."[3] This no doubt his *head* told him at one of the more major junctures in our era of dangerous politics, but his *impulses* remained pacifist. His ideal was to avoid armed combat, but not at the price of almost certain tyranny. Russell's most spectacular campaign on behalf of peace was his last—that culminating in non-violent direct action in the 1960s to promote British unilateral nuclear disarmament. Although not strictly a pacifist campaign, this one drew from Russell all that he contained of that "unbearable pity for the suffering of mankind."[4] He became a prophet of peace in a world addicted through fear to re-armament on even more terrifying levels than had occurred prior to two world wars. He ended life as a moral pathfinder in unmapped territory, trying to bring perspective where political leaders worried only over the next moves in the chess game of power. By his stand on the immorality of nuclear weapons, Russell introduced the moral imperative by which alone man has the possibility of surviving his technology.

What lay behind Russell's repeated endeavors to resolve political conflicts by peaceful means, to remove reliance on weaponry, and to live by the dual principles of reason and sensitivity to suffering? Surely the root of his pacifism is found in his "conversion" of early 1901, that experience of personal reorientation lying enigmatically at the heart of the first volume of his *Autobiography*. This turning-point in Russell's young manhood, this reorganization of his personality, has not been fully explained. Although this is told matter-of-factly in the narrative, the conversion can be seen as part of all later initiatives in social reform; but Russell himself seems to have been unable, or unwilling, to explain its full meaning in the context of his life. It is worth being reminded of exactly what he wrote:

> One day, Gilbert Murray came to Newnham to read part of his translation of *The Hippolytus*, then unpublished. Alys and I went to hear him, and I was profoundly stirred by the beauty of the poetry. When we came home, we found Mrs. Whitehead undergoing an unusually severe bout of pain. She seemed cut off from everyone and everything by walls of agony, and the sense of the solitude of each human soul suddenly overwhelmed me. Ever since my marriage, my emotional life had been calm and superficial. I had forgotten all the deeper issues, and had been content with flippant cleverness. Suddenly the ground seemed to give way beneath me, and I found myself in quite another region. Within five minutes I went through some such reflections as the following: the loneliness of the human soul is unendurable; nothing can penetrate it except the highest intensity of the sort of love that religious teachers have preached; whatever does not spring from this motive is harmful, or at best useless; it follows that war is wrong, that a public school education is abominable, that the use of force is to be depre-cated, and that in human relations one should penetrate to the core of loneliness in each person and speak to that. The Whiteheads' youngest boy, aged three, was in the room. I had previously taken no notice of him, nor he of me. He had to be prevented from troubling his mother in the middle of her paroxysms of pain. I took his hand and led him away. He came willingly, and felt at home with me. From that day to his death in the war in 1918, we were close friends.
>
> At the end of those five minutes, I had become a completely different person. For a time, a sort of mystic illumination possessed me. I felt that I knew the inmost thoughts of everybody that I met in the street, and though this was, no doubt, a delusion, I did in actual fact find myself in far closer touch than previously with all my friends, and many of my acquaintances. Having been an imperialist, I became during those five minutes a pro-Boer and a pacifist. Having for years cared only for exactness and analysis, I found myself filled with semi-mystical feelings about beauty, with an intense interest in chil-dren, and with a desire almost as profound as that of the Buddha to find some philosophy which should make human life endurable. A strange excitement possessed me, containing intense pain but also some element of triumph through the fact that I could dominate pain, and make it, as I thought, a gateway to wisdom. The mystic insight

which I then imagined myself to possess has largely faded, and the habit of analysis has reasserted itself. But something of what I thought I saw in that moment has remained always with me, causing my attitude during the first war, my interest in children, my indifference to minor misfortunes, and a certain emotional tone in all my human relations.[5]

The circumstances surrounding this extraordinary event are explained in a letter of 22 February 1912 (#354) to Lady Ottoline Morrell:

> I had just finished my greatest outburst of work, after the Congress in Paris at which I met Peano and began to know his writings [on notation]. I was feeling very triumphant, extraordinarily happy in work done, having been for months utterly oblivious of anything else. It was about six weeks after this that I had my first "conversion"; ever since then I have felt my technical work unsatisfying, not expressing the things I thought really important.

The meaning of Russell's first "conversion" was not interpreted by him much beyond this. I want to suggest that it came as the partial resolution of neurotic conflict, taking the form of what Henri Ellenberger calls a "creative illness." Ellenberger offers the concept of "creative illness" in *The Discovery of the Unconscious* (1970) to explain some of this century's leading psychological discoveries, chief among them Freud's discovery of the Oedipus complex and Jung's discovery of the archetypes of the unconscious. I believe that the concept "creative illness" also helps to explain Russell's acceptance of humanistic pacifism, which had for him the authenticity of a revelation. According to Ellenberger the main stages of a creative illness are as follows:

(1.) The beginning phase appears generally right after a period of intense intellectual effort, long reflection, meditations, or perhaps, too, after some work of a more technical nature, such as the research and accumulation of intellectual material.

(2.) During the illness, the subject is generally obsessed with a preoccupation that is dominant, which he will sometimes allow to appear, but which he often hides. He is preoccupied with the search for a thing or an idea, the importance of which he sets above everything.

(3.) The termination of the illness is experienced not only as the liberation from a long period of suffering, but as an illumination. The mind . . . is possessed by a new idea which he regards as a revelation, or a series of revelations. The cure is often so sudden that the subject cannot give the exact date of the occurrence. It is generally followed by a feeling of exultation, euphoria, enthusiasm, so intense that he may feel compensated in one stroke for his past suffering.

(4.) The cured illness is followed by a lasting transformation of personality. The subject has the impression of entering on a new life. He has made an intellectual or spiritual discovery which he will try hard to put to advantage: he has discovered a new world which during the rest of his life he will hardly be able to explore. If it is an idea, he will tend to present it as a universal truth; he will do so with so much conviction that he will succeed in having it accepted by others in spite of all difficulties.[6]

Ellenberger's idea of the self-healing creative illness is a distinctive secular rethinking of the idea of religious "conversion." It is consonant with the findings of Bennett and Nancy Simon.[7] According to the Simons, Russell affirmed pacifism—the doctrine of non-killing, of love toward all life and of doing good in evil situations—after an illumination of the meaning of human suffering. They rightly relate his deepened sense of human suffering to identification with the three-year-old Whitehead son at the time of his mother's angina attack—the immediate stimulus to Russell's transforming experience. The Simons point to Russell's actual loss of parents at about this age, but they do not use the term "creative illness" for the empathetic reaction which followed. His empathetic reaction was no doubt the dramatic manifestation of tensions that had been long incubated, as the psychologist William James described incubation. Russell's mystic illumination was probably the reparative phase of a long-incubated wish for integration of childhood feelings of loss and grief; the illumination made less disturbing the actualities of everyday living in which new instances of loss and grief occurred, or at least threatened to occur as in the case of Mrs. Whitehead.

This merging by "conversion" of inner and outer reality prepared the way for an eventual easing of the urgency of Russell's longing for a Platonic realm apart from ordinary life, a realm of pure number, of logical relations, untouched by the perturbations of life. The conversion humanized an escapist longing for mystical self-transcendence, the ecstatic moment paradoxically turning Russell back from the realm of pure logical and mathematical relations to that of human relations where the motivation arose in the first place. The illumination made him see the need to return to the world with a clearer sense of what needs doing here to heal the wounds of fate. Indeed, it put him into the reforming frame of mind which, he reports in the *Autobiography*, had characterized the lives of his long-lost parents, especially his mother. Russell generally reaffirmed their call for social justice, and when he speaks of wanting to base life on a philosophy as profound as that of the Buddha, it may be significant that his father had been a student of Buddhism. Russell's program of social reform, first fully elaborated in *Principles of Social Reconstruction* (1916), is thus deeply founded in his conversion and in awareness of his parents' social aims. With Russell's asceticism diminishing, with his retreat from Pythagorean mysticism, a new social consciousness arose based on humanistic pacifism. Coinciding with the end of the Boer War, his conversion did not have its fullest testing until the First World War when, to take a pacifist stand as Russell did, was to invite the scornful disapproval of the great majority of the British nation. Thus the conversion's durability was proved in action. As Russell wrote of his mathematical mysticism, "the non-human world remained as an occasional refuge, but not as a country in which to build one's permanent habitation."[8] The turn of pacifism was indeed the "spiritual discovery" which Russell's illumination of 1901 brought, his prophetic "new idea" with profound implications for his social involvement in two world wars and into the age of nuclear weaponry with its danger of global destruction.

THE HIPPOLYTUS

Let us look with more care at the factors which affected the secular form of Russell's conversion. What bearing did Gilbert Murray's reading of his translation of the *Hippolytus* have on it? As Russell says, he was stirred by the beauty of the poetry, an aesthetic reaction which led to a moral one. For Russell, aesthetic reactions were not enough; there had to be an overriding moral component before he could receive the consolation of beauty. The aesthetic force of the Greek play—its power to harmonize terrifying emotion—was a factor not to be underestimated in relation to Russell's marital tensions with Alys and difficulties in his technical work which preceded the conversion. Murray, the humanitarian and pacifist, was himself exemplary in the situation, but it was the content of his translation which prepared Russell to be deeply and constructively unsettled by Mrs. Whitehead's ordeal of the angina attack. To summarize, the *Hippolytus* concerns a fateful family imbroglio in which the malign goddess Aphrodite causes Phaedra, stepmother of Hippolytus, to fall in love with him because he is so innocent of sexuality. Phaedra resists the passion and is wrongly denounced by Hippolytus who believes his stepmother has designs on him. Shocked, Phaedra accuses Hippolytus of trying to violate her and hangs herself in despair. Cursed by his father, Hippolytus is dragged to death by runaway horses, but his innocence is revealed by Artemis, whose purity of motive contrasts with Aphrodite's malign sexuality.

Russell does not tell us exactly what he saw in this play, but it may be surmised that he identified with the wronged Hippolytus, innocent plaything of fate and subject to the will of a treacherous woman. Of the precise effect he wrote to Murray on 26 February 1901 only to say that he had "felt [the play's] power most keenly" and that Murray's poetry was "completely worthy of its theme." As to clues concerning what part, or parts, of the *Hippolytus* had most moved him, Russell remarks only that "I like best of all the lyric with which you ended your reading at Newnham. I learnt it by heart immediately, and it has been in my head ever since. There is only one word in it which I do not wholly like, and that is the word *bird-droves*." This word, he says, spoils the "peacefulness of the idea to my mind."[9] Murray's translation of the lyric spoken by the Chorus is as follows:

> Could I take me to some cavern for mine hiding,
> In the hill-tops where the Sun scarce hath trod;
> Or a cloud make the home of mine abiding,
> As a bird among the bird-droves of God!

Could I wing me to my rest amid the roar
Of the deep Adriatic on the shore,
Where the waters of Eridanus are clear,
And Phaëton's sad sisters by his grave
Weep into the river, and each tear
Gleams, a drop of amber, in the wave.[10]

But was this the only passage which stirred Russell to the depths? We do not know how much of the play Murray actually read, but we can guess that there were other more powerfully unsettling passages, such as Artemis's closing speech on vengeance (p. 72), which are likely to have touched Russell in the way he describes. The role of good and bad women in the play would certainly have been significant. The stepmother, tricked by a goddess's vicious whim, may have set up associations to his grandmother and aunt Agatha, dominant women in his life, though no special sexual threat is attributable to them. However this may be, the dismaying sense of uncontrolled family breakdown would have matched his feelings about the tragedy of his own family—that "gradual discovery, one by one, of the tragedies, hopeless and unalleviated."[11] A sense of meaningless loss and disintegration was aroused by the play just prior to Mrs. Whitehead's ordeal of the angina attack witnessed by her three-year-old son with whom Russell probably identified. But most important, in the legend of Hippolytus, the hero, torn apart by terrified horses on the seashore at Corinth, is restored to life and wholeness by Asclepius and renamed *vir bis*, or "twice a man." While not part of the play's action, Hippolytus's rebirth would not have escaped Murray. For Russell a cluster of isolated and confused feelings must have organized themselves into what may be called the "tragic view of life"—the view that sees heroic strivings laid waste by pride, or less explicably by fate, but yet redeemable in extremity even as Hippolytus was restored to life after unmerited suffering.

As the play gave formal containment to Hippolytus's tragedy, so Russell's conversion gave formal meaning to anguish over loss. (Conversion is as much a convention as is dramatic tragedy, with a form just as capable of leaving one with the feeling of "all passion spent.") Russell wrote to Murray of the play's effect: "Your tragedy fulfils perfectly—so it seems to me—the purpose of bringing out whatever is noble and beautiful in sorrow; and to those of us who are without a religion, this is the only consolation of which the spectacle of the world cannot deprive us."[12] Russell was without Christian consolation at least partly because he could not feel that justice prevails in a universe which wastes young lives such as those of his parents. But by realizing the hegemony of sorrow in his conversion, Russell acquired a new and deeply humane sort of religious feeling. Psychologically, the conversion put him in touch with his own depression, "converting" its pain, sadness, and anger into a world view which rendered these emotions less dangerous to his inner balance.

Unfortunately, Russell never found a fully satisfactory vehicle for the humanistic religion of sorrow, and feelings about it fluctuated through his life. A literary vehicle was attempted but proved inadequate in *The Pilgrimage of Life*, the brief meditations written in 1902–03 in which he tried to conjure back and reconcile himself to a personal past suffused with a sense of loss and sorrow. Something of what he hoped to achieve in literary meditation on the past may be gathered from a remark to G. Lowes Dickinson in a letter of 26 August 1902:

> Yes, one must learn to live in the Past, and so to dominate it that it is not a disquieting ghost or a horrible gibbering spectre stalking through the vast bare halls that once were full of life, but a gentle soothing companion, reminding one of the possibility of good things, and rebuking cynicism and cruelty.[13]

Russell's failure to effect "symbolic repair" in *The Pilgrimage of Life* meditations issued in the existential despair of "The Free Man's Worship" (1903)—one of this century's most profound literary statements of cosmic aloneness. To some readers the essay may verge on fatalism, but there is no doubt that it articulates Russell's pacifist revulsion against the cruelty of armed conflict, the position to which his conversion brought him. As Russell's statement of the pacifist position when it was new, "The Free Man's Worship" carries the imperative of looking on our fellow human beings as each alone and tragic.

> One by one, as they march, our comrades vanish from our sight, seized by the silent orders of omnipotent Death. Very brief is the time in which we can help them, in which their happiness or misery is decided.

> Be it ours to shed sunshine on their path, to lighten their sorrows by the balm of sympathy, to give them the pure joy of a never-tiring affection, to strengthen failing courage, to instil faith in hours of despair.[14]

This view as applied to war and peace was consistently held through the First World War. As to doing good actively through personal love, that was an area where much of Russell's confusion remained, an area which will be addressed separately; but we are concerned here only with his public witness in time of political strife as it followed from his conversion.

Conversion: The Nineteenth Century and After

Let us look further into the reasons why Russell's conversion took the secular, aesthetic, and moral form it did—setting aside the hope of help from Christianity. From adolescence Russell's thought about ultimate questions had undergone secularization, influenced by physics and the new biology. His loss of belief in the Christian account of creation and of human destiny (particularly in the doctrine of immortality of the soul) is chronicled in "Greek Exercises" (1888) and in "A Locked Diary" (1890–94). The entry for 31 August 1890 makes clear that Russell had been convinced by Mill's argument of the futility of asking "Who made God?" It is evident this early that Russell could not accept creative evolution as an alternative, and that he was headed toward agnosticism if not atheism, despite the inducement of ontological insecurity to believe otherwise. As he continues on 31 August 1890:

> To feel that the universe may be hurrying blindly towards all that is bad, that humanity may any day cease its progressive development and may continually lose all its fine qualities, that Evolution has no necessary progressive principle prompting it; these are thoughts which render life almost intolerable.[15]

We begin to see why it was that Russell's conversion preserved only the form not the content of the seventeenth-to-nineteenth-century Puritan tradition to which he belonged. The theistic content had already been bled away in the spiritual autobiographies of several of Russell's Victorian predecessors.

John Stuart Mill, Matthew Arnold, and Mark Rutherford, for

instance, all went through crises of losing belief with which Russell was familiar from reading their works. Mill was particularly close to Russell, having been a friend to his parents and becoming his "godfather" in a secular sense. The very upsurge of Victorian spiritual autobiography, seen at its best in that of Mill (1873), shows the self-help urge felt by those dispossessed of religion. Mill underwent a reparative experience when reading, in particular, Wordsworth's "Intimations of Immortality." Mill notes that Wordsworth also

> had felt that the first freshness of youthful enjoyment of life was not lasting; but that he had sought for compensation, and found it, in the way in which he was now teaching me to find it. The result was that I gradually, but completely, emerged from my habitual depression, and was never again subject to it.[16]

As Russell wrote to Lady Ottoline Morrell on 6 April 1911 (#19a), "Mill influenced me greatly and I lived on his autobiography for a time," although Wordsworth's pantheism was not as decisive for Russell as it had been for Mill.

A rebirth similar to Mill's also occurred in the life of Mark Rutherford, whose parents had been "rigid Calvinistic Independents." Rutherford (whom Russell noted to Lady Ottoline was "even better than I remembered . . . quite wonderfully sincere, and showing such a lovable man")[17] was converted to a sort of naturalistic pantheism by reading Wordsworth's *Lyrical Ballads*. Of this transformation Rutherford wrote:

> It excited a movement and a growth which went on till, by degrees, all the systems which enveloped me like a body gradually decayed from me and fell away into nothing. Of more importance, too, than the decay of systems was the birth of a habit of inner reference and a dislike to occupy myself with anything which did not in some way or other touch the soul.[18]

It is possible that Russell also read of Richard Jefferies' pantheistic enlargement of soul in *The Story of My Heart* (1883), and that his acquaintance with Count Tolstoy's conversion may have been influential. Under Victorian pressure of striving for purity of life, despite the breakdown of belief in revealed religion, and in the presence of a probable neurotic conflict, Russell's impetus to dra-

matic, non-theistic conversion became strong. Its aesthetic component is not as strange as at first might seem. In his chapter on ecstasy
in *Journey Through Despair 1880–1914*, John A. Lester points out that
turn-of-the-century spiritual despair often resolved itself by aesthetically induced ecstasy. Taking as their model the Romantics' most
cherished spiritual moments, as in the poetic ecstasies of Wordsworth
and Keats, writers as various as W. H. Hudson, Richard Jefferies,
Walter Pater, and Walt Whitman sought and found aesthetic moments through nature and art which helped to reconcile them to loss
of orthodox belief. Lester points out that the ecstatic aesthetic moment became the focal point of fictional art for such moderns as James
Joyce, Virginia Woolf, E. M. Forster, and W. B. Yeats. While
Russell's gift as an imaginative writer cannot be compared to theirs,
his desire for ecstatic experience can be assimilated to that found in
their writings.

Immediate to Russell's conversion of 1901 was the aesthetic
conversion of his brother-in-law and companion in Italy, Bernard
Berenson. It may be surprising to learn that Berenson, the hard-
driving art critic and dealer, should have undergone a spontaneous
and lastingly beneficial mental reorganization much as Mill and
Rutherford had known. Berenson's background was of course not
Christian but Jewish; yet the phenomenon of conversion is the same:
"a lasting and substantial mental reorganization, spontaneously
achieved and accepted as beneficial" as Marghanita Laski defines it.[19]
Berenson's biographers have neglected a profoundly important statement he makes in his essay on "Value," referring to a mystical
experience which occurred before 1900. After years of feeling that his
aesthetic reactions were lacking in attentiveness and depth,

> one morning as I was gazing at the leafy scrolls carved on the door
> jambs of S. Pietro outside Spoleto, suddenly stem, tendril, and foliage
> became alive and, in becoming alive, made me feel as if I had emerged
> into the light after long groping in the darkness of an initiation. I felt as
> one illumined, and beheld a world where every outline, every edge, and
> every surface was in a living relation to me and not, as hitherto, in a
> merely cognitive one. Since that morning, nothing visible has been
> indifferent or even dull. Everywhere I feel the ideated pulsation of
> vitality, I mean energy and radiance as if it all served to enhance my
> own functioning.[20]

This may be the fullest and most striking aesthetic ecstasy on record in the period, and it would be surprising if Russell had not heard it verbatim.

Russell first met Berenson at Friday's Hill (the Pearsall Smith's Sussex house) in the 1890s, and after their marriage he and Alys stayed with Berenson and his future wife, Alys's sister Mary, near Florence. This was in the spring of 1895; they were there subsequently when, for example, Russell began "The Free Man's Worship" at the Berenson villa, I Tatti, in December 1902. It is possible that Berenson communicated his aesthetically induced mystical experience on one or more of these occasions, and it may even have been discussed between them before Russell's own transformation of 1901.

Reinforcing these exposures to transformational spiritual and aesthetic experiences was Russell's probable awareness of William James's psychological studies of conversion. (We do not know for certain about this until 1 September 1902 when Russell wrote to Lucy Donnelly: "We have all been reading with great pleasure James on Religious Experience—everything good about the book except the conclusions."[21] James's theistic implications in the conclusions may have upset Russell—he does not tell us nor does he remark on whether he had had previous acquaintance with James's theories about religious experience.) In any case, James's Gifford Lectures of 1901 and 1902, entitled *The Varieties of Religious Experience*, touch on the main topics at issue in the experiences we have been looking at in creative illness: the sick soul, the divided self, incubation, and the soul's reunification by conversion. James's discussion is more specifically religious than the aesthetically induced experiences of Mill, Rutherford, and Berenson, but the processes he describes are similar. In Lecture IX on conversion James outlines what occurs in the transformation:

> To be converted, to be regenerated, to receive grace, to experience religion, to gain an assurance, are so many phrases which denote the process, gradual or sudden, by which a self hitherto divided, and consciously wrong, inferior and unhappy, becomes unified and consciously right, superior and happy, in consequence of its firmer hold upon religious realities.[22]

Russell kept up with James (having stayed with him in America in

1896) through Alys's family, the American Pearsall Smiths, with whom James was friendly. James's ideas about religion were discussed in the Pearsall Smith circle which dwelt upon conversion as part of experiential religion, as would be expected of such active late-Victorian Quaker evangelicals. It is possible that Russell was aware of these discussions. James is known to have admired the evangelical writer Hannah Pearsall Smith, Russell's mother-in-law, as "healthy-souled" and "realistic in her attitude to religion."[23]

That Russell came to dislike intensely Hannah Pearsall Smith does not imply that he ignored her views on religion, which were not as simple as one might suppose, thinking only of her evangelical activities. Indeed, Russell's critical attitude toward the mysticism to which he was inclined may well have been strengthened by her. Although she was brought up a Philadelphia Quaker, inured to the mystical expectations of silent worship, Hannah Pearsall Smith was not temperamentally attuned to listening for the still small voice of God. She confessed spending meetings for worship in childhood "building air castles" and entertaining grandiose fantasies about becoming "something very wonderful and grand," a preacher, inventor or singer.[24] *My Spiritual Autobiography* makes clear that Hannah was no mystic, and that she was in fact resistant to the religious elevation which makes for any sort of conversion: her mind got in the way. Hannah responded with feeling, however, to the "blessings of sanctification" claimed by Methodists when she and her husband Robert were converted from Quakerism during the evangelical revival of the 1870s. Before their removal to England, where as preachers they promoted "The Higher Life Movement," Hannah and Robert were converted by a "Baptism of the Spirit" in Methodist holiness meetings, but their conversions were very different.

Hannah experienced unaccustomed emotion in a prayer meeting when "the fountains of my being seemed to be broken up, and floods of delicious tears poured from my eyes," but by her own account she never enjoyed the full measure of "blessing" enjoyed by others. "I am not of an emotional nature, and none of the overpowering emotions I heard described, as constituting the 'blessing' ever fell to my portion," she wrote.[25] More depressive in temperament, Robert Pearsall Smith experienced the full effect of a camp meeting conversion and "came

home full of a divine glow that seemed to affect everybody he met."
He "had been shaken with what seemed like a magnetic thrill of
heavenly delight, and floods of glory seemed to pour through him,
soul and body, with the inward assurance that this was the longed-for
Baptism of the Holy Spirit."[26] The ecstasy lasted several weeks, giving
him charismatic power which in 1874 he took to England as an
evangelist. Robert's eventual fall from grace into the seductions of
"free love" which ruined his reputation is told by his son Logan in
Unforgotten Years and by Barbara Strachey in *Remarkable Relations*. He
never completely recovered equilibrium, and the taint remains still in
the Pearsall Smith family mythology.

It was undoubtedly Robert's sexual disgrace in 1875 which led
Hannah to write against all forms of fanatical religious conversion.
His father's misadventure certainly led Logan to write sneeringly in
his autobiography of his own childhood conversion at age four,
brought about by his sister Mary, age six. His mother, however, set
about correcting matters more systematically. Between 1890 and 1900
Hannah gathered a series of cautionary biographies showing that
delusions frequently underlie claims of sanctification. The collection,
remarkable for its time, is a genuinely skeptical reaction against the
excesses of religious emotion; its wry look at human behavior is not
unlike that found in some of Russell's later witty essays such as "Nice
People" (1931). Although Hannah's collection was not published
until 1928, Russell is known to have heard some of these cautionary
tales from her. He remarks in an autobiographical passage which
seems to reach back to 1896: "I remember an account written by my
mother-in-law of various cranks that she had known, in which there
was one chapter entitled 'Divine Guidance'. On reading the chapter
one discovered that this was a synonym for fornication."[27] Russell was
therefore aware of Hannah's skeptical view of what she called mysticism (she was thinking of the fanatical sorts of conversion, not of the
great Western mystics, Ruysbroeck, Tauler, or St. John of the Cross of
whose devotion she appears to have known little). Hannah wrote:

I would place at the entrance into the pathway of mysticism this
danger signal: Beware of impressions, beware of emotions, beware of
physical thrills, beware of voices, beware of everything, in short, that is

not according to the strict Bible standard and to your own highest reason.[28]

We would need to know the exact timing of Russell's exposure to Hannah's anti-mystical opinions to be sure what effect they had on his aesthetic and moral rather than religious conversion. It may be that his already tempered mysticism was deflected into secular channels by these stories, and that his trend toward anti-religion altogether was stimulated, not just by Hannah's cautionary tales, but by her forwardness as a religious writer whose powers of manipulation of persons were all too apparent to him. Russell came to think of her as "one of the wickedest people I had ever known," perhaps the cruellest words in his *Autobiography* (I, 148). She no doubt awakened antagonistic feelings toward his grandmother's religious and moral manipulations, fresh to recollection from the attempts Lady Russell had made to prevent his marriage to Alys. Russell's psychological *bête noir* was the controlling woman; yet the issue with which Hannah was concerned—reason protecting against excesses of religious emotion— was exactly the issue Russell developed in his later writings on religion. Russell's humanistic conversion would hardly have been that of a fanatic, so he could not fall under the severest of her strictures. It was an event of its time, coming between a dying evangelicalism and the rise of secular society whose artists and intellectuals were to discredit all but the immediate reference of creative insights, and whose psychologists would insist on studying creative insights. Russell was probably both excited and dismayed by Hannah's opinion of conversion, leading him to a quicker skeptical reaction than might have otherwise set in, the return of "the habit of analysis" as he put it. That Russell was an unwilling mystic at the fag end of a once vigorous Puritan tradition, we may thus in part attribute to Hannah Pearsall Smith; but I do not want to say that her influence was anything more than a nudge to his already skeptical intellect. Probably the pressure of Russell's creative illness was curbed and directed by Hannah's cautions, but he was in any case on guard against "enthusiasm," already that living paradox, the "passionate sceptic."

William James ended his lectures on *The Varieties of Religious Experience* feeling "almost appalled at the amount of emotionality which I find in it," having offered much "sentimental" and "extra-vagant" material which he studied rationally.[29] But Hannah Pearsall Smith had still more severe reservations than had James, as it is well to remember when speculating about the promptings to Russell's conversion. James was basically sympathetic to how the sick-divided soul is healed and reunified, and he gave the study of conversion intellectual respectability. It may be not only coincidence that Russell's humanistic transformation occurred just as the phenomenon of being "twice born" was under analysis by James in his Gifford Lectures. The matter deserves further study and should be placed in the still earlier context favorable to mysticism of the neo-Hegelianism of J. M. E. McTaggart and F. H. Bradley, to whose teachings Russell subscribed in the 1890s. The neo-Hegelian idealistic doctrine of the Absolute could well have encouraged mystical experience of at-oneness with the universe, a possibility which Russell could still entertain in *Prisons* and "The Essence of Religion" (1912). It was not until two years later in "Mysticism and Logic" that he criticized mysticism as distorting our view of the non-human world and as being unfit for the scientific philosophy he wanted. Thus Russell's changing view of mysticism, from his formal repudiation of neo-Hegelianism in 1898, needs to be considered along with the psychology of conversion.

Worth mention as a possible inducement to Russell's conversion is R. M. Bucke's *Cosmic Consciousness*, published in 1901 and perhaps known to Russell through the Pearsall Smiths. Bucke, a Canadian psychiatrist, was Walt Whitman's chief spokesman, and being on good terms with Whitman, it is likely that the Pearsall Smiths knew and discussed Bucke's advocacy of Cosmic Consciousness, whose highest exemplar was said to be the American poet. Bucke's book studies visionary ecstasies of famous and ordinary people from the Buddha, Plotinus, and Spinoza to recent persons identified only by initials. Pride of place is given to Whitman whom Russell had admired since the early 1890s, then as a sexual liberator but perhaps later as a seer and nature mystic.

Russell's enactment (however tempered) of the ecstatic experiences of which James and Bucke were talking complements the fact that typically conversions occur at about age thirty, the age of Christ at his baptism, of St. Augustine at his conversion, and of many seventeenth-century Puritans at theirs. So it is the catalyzing readiness in Russell that is at issue, not only direct influences. A set of factors, some of them deeply personal and hidden from Russell at the time, are involved. It would be misleading to pretend that influences alone tell the story of what seems to have been a "creative illness" which brought to the surface a regressive longing to re-experience the feelings of loss and grief that had been suppressed since Russell's childhood and became the sources of his "religion of sorrow," as he termed it to Lady Ottoline Morrell (June 1911, #98). His conversion was perhaps more a final common pathway for stressful feelings than it was a religious phenomenon in the sense understood by Hannah Pearsall Smith or by James when they wrote of conversion. Russell's conversion was a health-giving reorganization of psychological contents occasioned by the experience of literary tragedy and threatened actual loss in the lives of friends. Mrs. Whitehead's angina attack did more than awaken Russell to the apprehension of suffering and death which is the human lot; it broke what seems to have been an amnesia surrounding his feelings about the premature (and probably inadequately mourned) death of his parents and sister before he was four. In the best language available in 1901, Russell termed the crisis in his creative illness a "conversion." In making a humanistic pacifist of Russell, his spiritual crisis helped to open a moral pathway much needed by us as we contemplate far greater political perils of warfare than he did when in 1954 he warned of "man's peril."

Notes

1. "Man's Peril from the Hydrogen Bomb," *The Listener*, 52 (30 Dec. 1954), 1136.
2. "Earl Russell [Interviewed]," *Compass & Fleet*, 10 (Dec. 1964), 15.
3. *Autobiography, 1944–69* (New York: Simon and Schuster, 1969), III, 7.
4. *Autobiography*, I, 13.
5. Ibid., pp. 146–47. This account appears first on p. 83 of the dictated typescript of the *Autobiography*, dated May and June 1931. The holograph corrections to the typescript are few and do not change meaning. As far as is known, Russell did not record the conversion when it was fresh in 1901 but selected and pieced together the experience from memory thirty years later. This does not make the account suspect, but it does raise the problem as to whether all of the conversion's social implications fell together as neatly as they are made to seem to do in the later account. The experience of conversion was fictionalized in *The Perplexities of John Forstice* (1912), but Russell seems not to have imparted it otherwise unless by mention to Lady Ottoline Morrell. *See* Russell to Ottoline, 27 Dec. 1911 #300. In a letter of 13 Feb. 1912 to G. Lowes Dickinson Russell says that he has had just two mystical experiences, the first about ten years ago and another at the time of his "summer crises" with Lady Ottoline, which would have been mid- to late-July 1911. Russell's second conversion, not mentioned in the *Autobiography*, was the less dramatic, yet profoundly romantic and aesthetic change wrought by the love affair with Lady Ottoline. Its mysticism found expression in *Prisons*, a book Russell was unable to complete. *Prisons* bears the same relation to the second conversion as *The Pilgrimage of Life* bears to the first; both try to examine the implications of mystical experiences.

6. Henri F. Ellenberger, "The Concept of Creative Illness," *Psychoanalytic Review*, 55 (1968), 444. For a fuller discussion, see his *Discovery of the Unconscious* (London: Allen Lane, 1970).
7. Bennett and Nancy Simon, "The Pacifist Turn, pp. 11–24.
8. *My Philosophical Development*, p. 157.
9. Russell's letter to Murray is published in *Autobiography*, I, 156.
10. *The Hippolytus of Euripides*, trans. Gilbert Murray (London: George Allen & Unwin, 1902), p. 39.
11. *Autobiography*, I, 85.
12. Ibid., p. 156. It is noteworthy that when Russell wrote to Lady Ottoline

about his conversion (12 May 1911, #49), he commented that his wife, Alys, had not understood how meaningful it had been.

13. Published in *Autobiography*, I, 186.

14. "The Free Man's Worship" in *The Collected Papers of Bertrand Russell*, Vol. 12, pp. 71–72.

15. "'A Locked Diary'" in *The Collected Papers of Bertrand Russell*, Vol. 1, p. 56.

16. John Stuart Mill, *Autobiography* (London: Oxford University Press, 1924), p. 126.

17. Russell to Morrell, April 1913, #744. *See* Mark Rutherford, *Autobiography* (London: T. Fisher Unwin, 1896), p. 5, for the rigid Calvinistic parents.

18. Rutherford, *Autobiography*, pp. 18–19.

19. Marghanita Laski, *Ecstasy: A Study of Some Secular and Religious Experiences* (London: Cresset, 1961), p. 290. She discusses Berenson's experience.

20. Berenson, *Aesthetics and History in the Visual Arts* (New York: Pantheon, 1948), p. 72.

21. Published in *Autobiography* I, 165–67. James's comments on acceptance of God's will are used in an admonitory way in a letter of 14 September 1902 Russell wrote to the depressed Alys.

22. James, *The Varieties of Religious Experience* (London: Longmans, 1952), p. 186.

23. Quoted in Barbara Strachey, *Remarkable Relations* (London: Gollancz, 1980), pp. 72–73.

24. H. W. S. [Hannah Whitall Smith], *My Spiritual Autobiography or How I Discovered the Unselfishness of God* (New York: Fleming H. Revell Company, 1903), pp. 76–77.

25. Ibid., p. 286.

26. Ibid., p. 288.

27. *Autobiography*, I, 132–33.

28. Hannah Whitall Smith, *Religious Fanaticism*, ed. Ray Strachey (London: Faber & Gwyer, 1928), p. 164.

29. James, *Varieties of Religious Experience*, p. 476.

5

A Pathway Lost? The Problem of Mysticism

> Do not think it worth while to produce belief by concealing evidence, for the evidence is sure to come to light.
> —Bertrand Russell's Ten Commandments

The crisis of 1901 loosed psychic content which demanded to be dealt with—to be given form and meaning. A period followed during which Russell struggled to square this new knowledge with the shape of his life, his relational experience and his skeptical belief system. Russell confessed that "underlying all occupations and all pleasures I have felt since early youth is the pain of solitude." He added: "What Spinoza calls 'the intellectual love of God' has seemed to me the best thing to live by, but I have not had even the somewhat abstract God that Spinoza allowed himself to whom to attach my intellectual love. I have loved a ghost, and in loving a ghost my inmost self has itself become spectral."[1] It may be surprising that early in the century Russell's "vain search for God" had led him toward mysticism. Too late in the development of skepticism to be a Christian mystic, Russell nevertheless had a strong mystical urge which took several forms: Pythagorean mathematical mysticism, nostalgia for a lost past (being in love with a ghost), aesthetic feelings about nature and poetry and, finally, sensual and erotic mysticism. All offered experiences of high intensity calculated to dispel feelings of isolation and deprivation. His literary efforts prior to the Great War testify to largely futile attempts to reach sustained mystical consciousness. By following Russell's changing views of mysticism we see his emergence from asceticism to erotic activism—from spare mathematical Platonism to a Don Juan-like eroticism, not so unabashed as D. H. Lawrence's sexual apocalypticism but allied to it. A failed mystic, Russell was to become a prophet of sexual liberation, and I believe that his disppointed religious search and the continuing pain of isolation were the reasons.

To appreciate the strain that Russell put on mysticism as a concept we should be reminded of what traditionally mysticism has meant in the Christian West. For Dean W. R. Inge, writing in 1932 a preface to the seventh edition of *Christian Mysticism* (Bampton Lectures, 1899), mysticism is simply the purest form of prayer elevating the mind to God. Dean Inge's chief exemplars include not only St. John of the Cross, St. Teresa of Avila, and St. Francis of Assisi but also the Alexandrian Plotinus, whose *Enneads* helped to merge Platonism with Christianity. Purity of prayer, sometimes taking the form of ecstatic or visionary moments, transformed the lives of each of these mystics, leading to self-abandonment and an altered sense of reality. In *Mysticism* (1910) Evelyn Underhill describes the stages of disciplined awareness through which the mystic typically passes: awakening, purification, illumination, introversion, the dark night of the soul, and a final unitive state fulfilling the journey to God as light and love. Underhill's historical analysis of the mystic way is documented with examples from St. Paul and the author of the Fourth Gospel to William Blake, the late eighteenth-century poet, painter, and prophet. Together, these books establish norms for mystical awareness, shown to have been the outcome of only a very few privileged lives over the centuries.

Let us review Russell's quest for religious truth by looking at the origins of what may be called his ontological insecurity, at his conversion of 1901 and the writings following from it, preceding those associated with his "second conversion" during the love affair with Lady Ottoline Morrell. Nature mysticism is seen as early as 1888 in the "Greek Exercises," with mysticism remaining a central theme in writings on religion until his early forties when, in "Mysticism and Logic," he all but repudiated it in making the case for logic as the key to truth. But even in that essay the account of mysticism is surprisingly sympathetic.

So vehement an anti-Christian as Russell would not be expected to value mystical experience. The sharp debating points of "Why I Am Not a Christian" (1927) hardly recall his earlier anguished search for religious truth within the Christian church followed by his search for non-dogmatic forms of mysticism. A secularized language of mysticism was, however, always with him, as in the final paragraph of his *Autobiography*:

> I have lived in the pursuit of a vision, both personal and social. Personal: to care for what is noble, for what is beautiful, for what is gentle; to allow moments of insight to give wisdom to more mundane times. (III, 223)

In his strenuous anti-Christian moods, as in debate with Father Copleston on the existence of God (1948), Russell allowed that while he saw no reason to think that religious experience proved the existence of God, it could improve moral character. As he put it, "I've had experiences myself that have altered my character profoundly. And I thought at the time at any rate that it was altered for the good. Those experiences were important, but they did not involve the existence of something outside me." [2] As early as "Seems, Madam? Nay, It Is" (1897), Russell had made exactly this point: "The value of the [religious] experiences in question must . . . be based wholly on their emotional quality, and not, as Bradley would seem to suggest, on any superior degree of truth which may attach to them."[3] Indeed in "On the Distinction between the Psychological and Metaphysical Points of View" (c. 1894) Russell had cautioned about the vague feelings conjured up in F. H. Bradley's doctrines and about the danger of plunging into mysticism.[4] "The Free Man's Worship" (1903) states the need for stoicism in the realization "[t]hat Man is the product of causes which had no prevision of the end they were achieving," that we "are but the outcome of accidental collocations of atoms."[5] Though we may "burn with passion for eternal things," it is unlikely that intuition will unlock the universe's secrets.[6] The point about the moral good of mystical contemplation was repeated in *Mysticism and Logic* (1914) and also appeared in a review of Dean Inge's *The Philosophy of Plotinus* (1919).

By the time Russell went up to Cambridge in 1890 he had jettisoned the Christian metaphysic of his childhood, including the doctrine of the soul's immortality (see *Collected Papers*, I, 47). But he was still susceptible to the appeal of systems showing that the universe cares for man, as neo-Hegelianism seemed to say. Neo-Hegelianism was the dominant philosophy at Cambridge and Russell briefly adhered to "the Absolute," a metaphysical term more suggestive of mysticism than of empiricism. However, about 1897, influenced by G. E. Moore, Russell gave up the doctrines of Bradley, the Oxford philosopher, and of his Cambridge tutor, J. M. E. McTaggart, whose form of idealism no longer seemed tenable. But Russell could never rid himself of idealism altogether, with his investigations into the philosophy of mathematics always having some background of it. As he said: "I came to think of mathematics . . . as an abstract edifice subsisting in a Platonic heaven and only reaching the world of sense in an impure and degraded form."[7] He longed for a sort of nirvana of number, a revelation of the eternal transcending the forms of time. In "The Study of Mathematics" (1907) he speaks of the "supreme beauty" and "stern perfection" of its demonstrations, affirming the power of reason to delineate a realm of the ideal.[8] Disillusioned, he wrote in 1959, "I cannot any longer find any mystical satisfaction in the contemplation of mathematical truth," but in the early years of the century his hope had the strength of a metaphysical hunger.[9] The complications of human relations both urged him to take refuge in abstractions and pulled him away from them when moral claims became too much to avoid.

In February 1901 Russell underwent what he called a "sort of mystic illumination," prompting a tenderness toward suffering humanity and setting aside, if only temporarily, the "habit of analysis" (*Autobiography* I, 146). The conversion emerged from an aesthetic experience of Greek tragedy followed by an empathetic response to Mrs. Whitehead's acute suffering in an angina attack. Russell was prompted to think of the "solitude of each human soul" and to identify with Mrs. Whitehead's young son who had to be taken from his mother's side. From the fact that Russell was moved so deeply and, as he claimed, permanently transformed by the insight, we may infer that repressed feelings had been activated. It is probable that the event pierced defenses against grief and sorrow for the deaths of his parents and sister before he was four. The altered state of consciousness dramatically changed what he thought life was about, preparing for humane endeavors in the world rather than maintaining exclusive commitment to the technical problems of philosophy. The conversion's effect was to validate intuition as a way of knowing in the moral realm, but over time it had some curious results.

II

The first literary result of Russell's transformed consciousness in the conversion was *The Pilgrimage of Life* (1902–3). These twenty-one lyrical prose meditations may well have been attempts to resume the mourning process for his lost parents and sister; their melancholy and pessimism suggests origins in the writer's own preoccupation with an unreachable past. They are written in a language of the soul shunning an inhospitable world and looking to the moral compensations of courage, love, and peace as possibilities for man, qualities not inherent in a universe lacking the certainty of God. Typifying the condition of radical spiritual loss, Russell wrote: "We are all orphans and exiles, lost children wandering in the night, with hopes, ideals, aspirations that must not be choked by a heartless world."[10] He examines in his own case the perception of the conversion that "the loneliness of the human soul is unendurable" (*Autobiography*, I, 146), asking radical questions about our ultimate support in a universe devoid, as it seemed to him, of God. His consolation is less than might be wished: nature "speaking straight to experience and sorrow" and "eternal beauty . . . ready to stanch the wounds which man inflicts on man."[11] The darker shades of melancholia in these writings do not yield to such glimmers of hope. Mystical transformation is more discussed than enacted as in the meditation on "Religion," while the psychological issues of grief, sadness, and mourning are never quite brought to the surface where they could be confronted and perhaps healed rather than projected as cosmic pessimism. No doubt the attempt at imaginative closure with the painful past gave some relief, but the contact was not one he could sustain, leading as it would to painfully dichotomized feelings of loss and rage. The struggle would not then have been between reason and emotion, as is often maintained of Russell, but between repressed contending emotions from which no easy deliverance could be envisaged. As far as is known, *The*

Pilgrimage of Life was abandoned incomplete, with its self-analytic mode of psychic survival largely discredited. His vision of man alone in an uncaring universe prompted an appeal to something more reassuringly personal, and it is not to be wondered that, with the failure of his marriage to Alys Pearsall Smith, Russell should find other companionship. In 1911 he began an affair with Lady Ottoline Morrell which stimulated the next two stages of Russell's mysticism, the Spinozistic and the erotic.

III

Russell's affair with Lady Ottoline was an adventure in expanding the sensibilities, centering as it did on a quest for beauty in nature and the arts. Religious questions, however, were to bring strife. One can find in the polarizing conflict revealed in their love letters the explanation for Russell's most remarkable psychological discovery about the split nature of the human psyche. Like the great imaginative writers, Shakespeare in *The Tempest* and Milton in *Paradise Lost*, for instance, Russell hit upon the bipolar archetype as his central organizing image in *Prisons*. Remarkable though this writing sometimes is, regrettably his powers of imaginative creation are not up to the core material in *Prisons*, material derived from contact with the conflicted psyche, the author's own inner division. The exercise was intellectual, to unify the opposites discovered in the confrontation of two different personalities. Russell wanted a product of the physical union between himself and Lady Ottoline, and the book *Prisons* was to be their "child." Thus the act of writing was itself a symbolic unification—of male with female, unbelief with belief—into a non-theistic mystical tract.

In contrast to the cosmic loneliness of "The Free Man's Worship," *Prisons* sees the universe as abounding in opportunity for self-enlargement through impersonal contemplation and love. "The essence of religion is union with the universe achieved by subordination of the demands of Self," Russell wrote.[12] The high-minded ascetic demand contrasts with the sensual delights spoken in the love letters, and we do not know that Russell ever entered upon the austerities implied in his new view of religious purpose. Nonetheless, he writes of striving for a monistic contemplative attitude independent of beliefs about the actual nature of the universe, a sort of "cosmic consciousness" without a supporting metaphysic. The teaching of *Prisons* is one of emotional self-help, of a sort of purgation to achieve a purified state of mind, setting aside action in favor of contemplation. This was to prepare for a sort of "communion of saints," as the outline for this incomplete work puts it.

The title *Prisons* probably reflects the chapter in Spinoza's *Ethics*, "Of Human Bondage, or the Strength of the Emotions." To Russell, *Prisons* meant incarceration of the self, an idea carrying over the personal anguish of *The Pilgrimage of Life*.[13] Mysticism as a delving into the painful personal past seems to have been too much to sustain, and the new writing strives for impersonality. Self-imprisonment prevents contact with external revivifying forces in the universe of Spinoza's pantheistic visions: "Self, children, friends, country, all prisons," Russell wrote in an outline.

> What is [a] prison? Self-interest, subjectivity, insistence. Why a prison? because [it] shuts out the love, the knowledge, and the attainment of goods otherwise possible.[14]

The universe, he adds, "forbids the freedom of omnipotence; it permits the freedom of contemplation"; that is, it is unnatural for anyone to want ultimate control over his environment and the people in it. Contemplation counteracts egotism, freeing and reassuring the lonely soul. Thus Russell talks about the essential schizoid problem of withdrawal out of fear of there being nothing there, a fear poignantly pictured in "The Free Man's Worship." The weakened schizoid ego may well imagine an empty universe, devoid of caring, and, in compensation, try to build a system of necessary intellectual dependencies which make the universe less frightening. But mathematics and logic are too inhuman to be completely satisfying even to an intellect so large as Russell's. Spinoza's austere intellectuality applied to questions of human meaning was a reassuring model by which to reappraise the erotic feelings aroused by Lady Ottoline.

Spinoza clearly delineates the psychology of selfhood which by enslavement to passion and loss of inner harmony prevents true freedom. He wrote, "In so far as men are prey to passion they cannot, in that respect, be said to be naturally in harmony" (Book IV, Prop. XXXII).[15] Assailed by his passions, man is, "variable and inconstant" (Bk. IV, Prop. XXXIII), and these variable passions "can be contrary to one another" (Bk. IV, Prop. XXXIV). It would be more than two centuries before this insight about inner division would become known in psychodymanic theory as "splitting." In *Studies in Hysteria* (1893–95) Freud outlined splitting of the ego as a process which seriously weakens the individual's capacity to face life confidently. Since Freud, the concept of ego-splitting has been elaborated, for instance by W. R. D. Fairbairn, to explain the divided-against-oneself feeling that poorly integrated people struggle against. The cause of ego-weakness, appearing when defensive functions are less than effective, is said to reflect "splitting" of the ego into antithetical part structures. These are traceable to "good" and "bad" experiences with parents at the beginning of life. If the parents have been lost early, as happened to Russell, there is bound to be residual depressiveness. When, in addition, the substitute caretaking is domineering, as that given by Russell's grandmother, conditions are set for a turbulent and rebellious ego. The resulting inner division is certainly capable of later modification, of which one means is symbolic integration by mathematical speculations and mystical vision. I see Russell's pattern-making in this era, heightened by good and bad romances, as having an ego-reparative intention, his literary efforts directed toward proving to himself that a unified configuration could contain split and contending elements. These elements, simultaneous desire and fear of capture, the stuff of his "second conversion" stimulated by Lady Ottoline, typify the unstable romantic alliance and ease the pain of being together. Time and again Russell admitted to injuring what he most loved.

> I have spoilt another opportunity—put another nail in the coffin of former joys—but life is long, and the battle is not lost—it is never lost till death. I *will* win through in the end—and never never will I give up the fight with Satan. . . . I love you with such an aching love—when I hurt you, all the tragedy of the world seems condensed into one dreadful thing—and yet I go on, and hurt you again and again. Why? I don't know—it is a mystery to me. And all the while the greatness of love remains in my heart, though I sin against it. (#814, 21 January 1913)

This is precisely the passionate disharmony Spinoza identified in the seventeenth century as most deeply troubling to the human heart. In *The Perplexities of John Forstice* (1912), a novella whose discussion of attitudes to life turns upon the protagonist's guilt about his ailing wife, mysticism's relief from fearful contraries is again considered in the statement of Nasispo, whose name was intended as an anagram for Spinoza. Nasispo speaks of a realm of pure Being to which the contemplative may aspire, leaving behind all hopes and fears. Wrapt into "Spinoza's intellectual love of God, that 'infinite love with which God loves himself'," the contemplative is freed of all worldly desire; but was this an actual possibility for Russell?[16] Another voice of his divided inner state, Chenskoff the Russian novelist, puts the matter more realistically. Chenskoff complains of human relations not satisfying his craving for beauty and speaks of "the infinite pain that lies at the heart of life"—the source of all great achievement, as it is said.[17] (Of all the speakers in *Forstice*, Chenskoff enunciates most clearly Russell's view of creativity as pursuit of a "vision beyond our reach," an essence of being that we need in order to be whole.) He goes on to sound very much like the Russell of *Pilgrimage* when he speaks of "escape from the pursuing spectre," of "the terrible sorrows of childhood," and of having to learn acceptance of "the deepest horror in the dark caverns of the Soul"—perhaps the empty space left by unmourned losses.[18] But here the fictive voice can change the subject, as indeed happens in Part III, Forstice's uncle's love story.

To return to *Prisons*, "Action and Contemplation" explains the monism of contemplation as not dividing "objects into two opposed camps," which would be the way of power. Rather it is the way of wisdom Russell wishes to follow, enlargement of soul to reach a unity of action impregnated by contemplation. The essay ends with a poetic figure commending love as our highest good and seeing its object "as part of the whole ocean of Being," reminiscent of the "oceanic feeling" of which Romaine Rolland spoke to Freud.[19] "Freedom and Bondage" seems to qualify this oceanic vision by saying that contemplative freedom is never complete, that desire always limits it, a significant confession in view of the emerging sexual mysticism, precursor of his phase as propagandist for a relaxed sexual morality. Desire and freedom from bondage increasingly take on primacy in Russell's thought about sexuality, with the spiritual objective of "union with the universe" fading into the background of idealism about which he chose to say less as his relational life grew more complicated.[20] Since the intended order of *Prisons* is conjectural, it is impossible to say that the idealistic passages on "The Good" were meant to close the writing. As it stands, they determine the tone of the whole, dealing in "Wisdom" with reconciliation of "two souls in man," the animal and the divine. Reason is invoked to mediate man's inner conflicts, but the writing is inconclusive. All that Russell wished to say on the subject he summarized in the final paragraphs of "The Essence of Religion," the last of his published statements partial to mysticism.

Russell's self-teaching in *Prisons* did not carry him very far toward the integration of ego his tormented love affair with Lady Ottoline told him he needed. Spinozistic conceptions are too rarefied to touch the psychological issues that emerged: unmet dependency needs and acute sexual ambivalence. *Prisons* may be mainly wishful thinking, an attempt to escape inner pain by means of Spinoza's ethical system with which Russell hoped Lady Ottoline would merge her Christian beliefs. Their involvement, and his ego needs in particular, were too complex for the attempted reparative function of this writing. Russell speaks of a contemplative world of freedom where "the worst sorrows do not survive," but what were these sorrows; did he have to leave them so substanceless when, as his letters to Lady Ottoline show, spiritual autobiography was his true literary metier?[21] Russell was obsessed with trying to draw the essence of spirituality out of his all too human experience: he wanted to record once and for all the route to truth, but he lacked a language in which to speak of relationship and sexuality—a lack he would try to make good in the next phase of his mystical search. *Prisons* remains at the level of abstraction, enquiring into ideal unity, brilliantly symbolizing dualism within the ego but failing to enunciate a new religion of love and reason.

IV

There was a pre-Great War revival of mystical religion in England nurtured by such people as Dean Inge and Evelyn Underhill. The war pushed this into the background, and Russell's concern with the topic subsided; after "Mysticism and Logic" he had little to say about it.[22]

The war loosened conventional morality, with Russell himself entering upon another love affair with Lady Constance Malleson. The Bloomsbury emphasis on relationships took over the asceticism, leading to Russell prescribing his liberal view in *Marriage and Morals* (1929). A sort of coital mysticism is implicit, and anxiety about potency is detectable in this and related popular writings: but the tone of *Marriage and Morals* is that of objective social science designed to banish superstition and prejudice from the free sexual adventures most young people are assumed to want. Russell became increasingly favorable in his notices of such sexual liberators as Margaret Sanger, Edward Carpenter, and Havelock Ellis. The "longing for love" with which Russell heads up his list of objectives in "What I Have Lived For" (*Autobiography*, I, 13) displaced the stringent moralism of a Victorian upbringing. Was his affirmation of sexuality not a negation of all he had hoped for from Spinoza's "intellectual love of God"? Or does it show that mysticism was only a replaceable sublimation of the sexual behavior he all along wanted to enact?

Russell well knew that the traditional mystics' desires for direct union with God were often spoken of in orgasmic language, and that aim-inhibited sexuality had much to do with austerity in the cloister. He himself stated that mysticism "is primarily a sublimation of sex."[23] Perhaps the traumatic public events of the early part of this century led to cynicism about the motives for self-regulation which historically had redirected biological urges into spiritual channels. Self-expression and self-gratification came too rapidly to the fore, with Russell easily moving into the vanguard of a changed morality. The liberationists' cry for release from monogamy could not envisage the amount of anguish for interpersonal damage that a too quick relaxation of the rules would cause. Surely there can be few cases on record of so rapid an alteration of course as Russell's from mystical ascetic to sponsor of permissive sexuality. His four marriages, numerous liaisons, and propaganda for easier divorce seem to cancel from the record his earlier mysticism. He became captive of an anti-Spinozistic sexual passion, almost a caricature Don Juan adrift in a world without moral bearings. He could find no justification for other than a relativistic ethics. It is easy to condemn him as a harbinger of the age of narcissism, which no doubt he would have deplored in its full-blown state. Russell found it impossible to be a mystic in any accepted meaning of the term. The pain of solitude which he suffered was no doubt assuaged but never removed by his mystical longings and experiences. He could not be a creative writer either, striving for epiphanies and "moments of being" through the fictive voice as did, for instance, James Joyce and Virginia Woolf. Undoubtedly Russell's brush in 1901 with a truer form of mysticism survived in his wish for a warless world, but his more immediate direction lay down the garden path.

Notes

1. Russell, *Autobiography* II, 38.
2. Russell, *Why I Am Not a Christian*, p. 158.
3. *Cambridge Essays, 1888–99*, p. 110.
4. Ibid., p. 196.
5. *Contemplation and Action, 1902–14*, pp. 66–67.
6. Ibid., p. 71.
7. Russell, *My Philosophical Development*, p. 155.
8. *Contemplation and Action*, p. 86.
9. *My Philosophical Development*, p. 157.
10. *Contemplation and Action*, p. 42. Russell's view of mystical contemplation as retrieval of the past owes much to his reading of the Belgian Symbolist Maurice Maeterlinck's *Le Temple Enseveli*, as he explained to Helen Flexner in a letter of 2 August 1902.
11. Ibid., pp. 43, 47.
12. *Contemplation and Action*, p. 105.
13. Ibid., cf. p. 40.
14. Ibid., p. 102.
15. Benedict de Spinoza, *The Ethics*, trans. R. H. M. Elwes (New York: Dover, 1955), p. 207.
16. *Contemplation and Action*, p. 138.
17. Ibid., p. 140.
18. Ibid., pp. 141–2
19. Ibid., pp. 103–4.
20. Ibid., p. 108.
21. Ibid., p. 103.
22. Russell's changing view of mystical experience appears in such letters to

Lady Ottoline as # 176, 342, 427, and 1,321. For a psychiatric view of mystical experience as adaptive see Paul C. Horton, M.D., "The Mystical Experience as a Suicide Preventive," *American Journal of Psychiatry*, 130 (March 1973), 294–96.

23. "On Bad Passions," in *The Philosophy of Logical Atomism and Other Essays, 1914–19*, ed. J. G. Slater, Vol. 8 of the *Collected Papers* (London and Boston: Allen and Unwin, 1986), p. 274.

CHAPTER

6

Romantic Attachments and Illusions: Love Letters

The great source of terror in infancy is solitude.
—William James, *Principles of Psychology.*

Russell the philosopher, in his passion for exact logical and mathematical truth, has been rightly likened to Faust, a likeness he accepted. The passions governing his life Russell treats in "What I Have Lived For": "the longing for love, the search for knowledge, and unbearable pity for the suffering of mankind." The first is the subject of what follows. To speak, as Russell did in his autobiography (I, 13), of love that "brings ecstasy—ecstasy so great that I would often have sacrificed all the rest of life for a few hours of this joy," a love that "relieves loneliness," suggests that beyond the Faust legend is another still more pertinent. This is the legend of Don Juan searching for the ultimately fulfilling love object. In the Romantic period Faust legends combined with those of Don Juan, who was seen to be more melancholic and divinely discontented than wicked. Russell was a moral Don Juan, never intending evil but driven by the desire to know the truth and by hunger for a perfect unaltering love. Alistair Cooke remarks that Russell "might in a mellow moment . . . have admitted that lechery was a curse and got men into situations that came to entail impossible involvements."[1] We will study these involvements in three of Russell's love correspondences, those with his first wife, Alys Pearsall Smith, Lady Ottoline Morrell, and Lady Constance Malleson.

In a brief essay of 1932 entitled "Our Women Haters," Russell considers the problem of Don Juan, with whom he professes to have "little patience." The Don Juan is "perpertually seeking his ideal in

95

Woman, failing to find it, and abandoning the flawed idol as soon as he perceives the flaw."[2] Russell caricatures the type, asking why any man or woman should ever be idealized. He does not hint that the term might, in some way, apply to himself, a self with which he often indeed had "little patience." Russell might have admitted to abnormally strong sexual urges, but not to Don Juanism. Yet as we shall see in chapter 8, it is an essential characteristic in the very moral make-up which accounts for his being so significant a prophet in our time.

The nature of Russell's relations with women is perhaps best seen in his extensive love correspondences, where both his own strengths and inadequacies and the current lady's attractions and flaws could be distanced. Psychological distance seemed necessary to Russell, on occasion allowing him those "moments of being" the creative writer of Bloomsbury vintage most desired. Part fiction, part self-revelation, the best of his letters reach an aesthetic level unattained by him in any other literary form. Not to discount the vibrancy of direct encounters, there is a special quality in the correspondence which Russell himself recognizes when he writes to Lady Ottoline Morrell (#394) that "We get something from letters that we should not get otherwise—the deeper things come out, and I think you say things you would hardly say in talk."

Before discussing the love correspondences themselves it should be said that Russell was very aware of the art of letter writing. While attracted to such aggressively "modern" fiction writers as D. H. Lawrence and Joseph Conrad (both of whom figure prominently in the letters to Ottoline), Russell remained Victorian in his taste for clear but elegant statement. As was natural in the cultivated aristocratic Victorian society in which he grew up, the letter served both to convey necessary information and to give evidence of good breeding. A well-bred person was expected to be able to write good letters that said what they meant with a happy turn of phrase. He wrote in the preface to *Dear Bertrand Russell . . .: A Selection of His Correspondence with the General Public* (1969). "In my youth it was imperative to master the art of letter-writing if one was to make one's way in the world." While ridiculing the excesses of formality, Russell is quite definite in these remarks that letter-writing was a socially necessitated art, now regrettably lost.

Behind this again was the eighteenth-century epistolary vogue by which the reading public learned of the witty eloquence of, say, Horace Walpole, or of the power to affect of the depressive poet William Cowper. By the nineteenth century, an intellectual letter writer such as J. S. Mill could expect his correspondence to find its way to a considerable readership. Russell, it appears, was an eager letter reader, though probably first attracted to Mill the person, his god-father, through the *Autobiography* published in 1873 and then reintroduced to him when the letters appeared in 1910. Russell modified letter-writing of Mill's sort toward a penetrating self-analytical candor, an ability to govern and discuss even while displaying the strong feelings that sometimes threatened to overwhelm him. To do this he must certainly have given thought to the letter as art—a means of revealing and preserving in safety the emotional truth of his new relationships as they unfolded. The idea of eventual publication made the confessional impulse complete.

When Russell came to prepare his *Autobiography* for publication some years after drafting it, he included a variety of letters to convey the immediacy of situations noticed in the narrative, thus upholding the letter in its own right. It is remarkable how many mentions there are in his corpus of the correspondence of other distinguished letter-writers. Mentioned in the letters to Ottoline are letters by Keats, Shelley, Dostoevsky, Tchaikovsky, Beethoven, and Mme. du Deffand who corresponded with Walpole and Voltaire. These correspondences are frequently judged for their leavening effect on Russell's mind and are discussed along with other literature and arts as agents of the metamorphosis he was undergoing. Having such a high standard made him critical of his earlier letter-writing and of the self it represented. He considers critically (in #529) his old letters returned by Alys, disliking the contemptuous tone they shared toward people in general and feeling himself to have been excessively critical to her. Russell knew that letters disclose the person at his or her most essential, and he wanted to be under no illusions about the changes they represent. He reports reading through his mother's letters, given to him by T. J. Cobden-Sanderson, looking for evidences of her character, a task in which Lady Ottoline participated. (In 1937 he published *The Amberley Papers*, their letters, as a memorial to the brief lives of his parents; the editorial task was shared by his third wife, Patricia Spence.) But most important are his comments on his own letters as literary efforts worth preserving. For example, in letter #322 he appeals to Ottoline to "find any old letters of mine that seem to have bits that will do: I write better in letters, it seems to me." "Bits that will do," it appears, were choice prose extracts displaying his powers at their best on topics they had been discussing. Then or later Ottoline set about marking what seemed the most impressive passages, such as the striking meditation on the River Thames in letter #87. These markings show consistently good judgment, though as the affair's plot thickens the marked passages are the personal ones, not simply examples of literary excellence.

We turn to the letters themselves, beginning with those written during the courtship of Russell's first wife. His early letters to Alys Pearsall Smith are filled with romantic ardor. She for her part was less ardent, giving only gradual assent to his wish for marriage. In Paris (where his grandmother had persuaded him to take a temporary diplomatic post, which she hoped would cool his passion for Alys) Russell fantasized the perfect relationship marriage would bring. The only problem was an immediate one: to win over Granny, whom he says he honors almost to idolatry (17 November 1893). We would not expect the goading but censuring internalized Granny to be mentioned. There is a great diversity of interest in Russell's letters from Paris. They show his mind developing its philosophical ambition as awesome powers of thought find direction, but as personal documents they reveal illusory hopes—a love vision restlessly unsure of itself, steeped in sexual anxiety, yet unshakably confident that marriage will perfect every imperfection. He looks for release from a crushing sense of solitude and isolation, a feeling that if he were known as he knows himself he would be despised as he despises himself (17 December 1893). Russell invents an Alys as much as he writes to her. He had to win himself away from an Alastor-like passion for a phantom created by his own imagination, as he says (30 September 1894). She is his bridge from the enclosed mind to the outside world. Alys functioned very well in the world, with her temperance-speaking and advanced opinions on social issues of the day. Her convictions were not so far from

Granny's moral sanctions, but, as an American, she offered Russell an escape from English Victorian straightness, just as psychologically she (temporarily) relieved him of isolation and fear. The union, Russell is convinced, will be beautiful and permanent, yet ominously he requires independence (21 January 1894), though acknowledging the greatest dependence on her. She in fact speaks of mothering him, of loving him as if he were her child as well as being her lover and great inspiration (28 October 1894). The danger of his recoil from mothering is as plain as his desire for it. That the repulsion was due to an insidiously internalized Granny is strongly suggested in remarks on fear of her death, which Russell chose to quote in his *Autobiography*. (We recall that Lady Russell used ill health to control him.)

> I realize that thee and I together were trying to stamp out my affection for my Grandmother, and that the attempt was a failure. My conscience was bad, so that I dreamt about her every night, and always had an uneasy consciousness of her in the background of even the happiest moments. Now, if she dies, I shall have a good conscience towards her: otherwise I should have had, I believe for life, the worst sort of remorse, the remorse for cruelty to a person whom death has removed from one's longing to make up for past deficiencies. My love for her is altogether too real to be ignored with impunity. . . . (I, 101)

The breakdown of Russell's long marriage to Alys crushed her spirit. She was the loser more than he, but her letters during treatments for depression in 1902 show how disillusion had deepened on both sides. She apologizes for eight years of doing him harm (15 September 1902). Alys was always too self-effacing, too ready to accept blame for what went wrong in her life. Her mental abilities hardly matched Russell's but at her best she was concerned, sincere, and intuitive, though the unseeing prisoner of her own complicated family life. (Both mother and father were Quaker preachers, with her mother the dominant force, especially after her father had been discredited by sexual excesses in connection with his evangelism in England.) Much of Alys's side of the correspondence concerns Pearsall Smith family affairs, with now and then a glimpse of Russell's involvement, as when he enjoyed consorting in Paris with her more glamorous and worldly sister "Mariechen," later wife of the art critic Bernard Berenson. Thus early we see an example of Russell's unending quest for the stimulus of changing female companionship. Alys does not catch the implication, or at least does not say so directly. With an occasional exception, her letters show little power of reflection, little sense of just where things might go wrong. A striking exception is in a letter of 8 October 1894 where Alys reports to Russell a premonitory dream: she and Bertie were married and she was lying in his arms in perfect bliss and happiness, except for the disturbing feeling that it was not real. In the dream she reported this feeling to Bertie, who replied that it must be real because he so desired it to be. She was shocked by her lover's appearance: instead of looking intellectual and distinguished he had repulsive brown eyes and a sinister curling moustache. Bertie told her with a silly grin that he had had another photograph taken to please her. In the morning the photograph on Alys's desk reassures her that her lover has not the features of personality intuition tells her he has. She had glimpsed a stage villain, a persecutor of weakness in women, only to wish him away.

To her credit, Alys had realistically chided Russell for too much romantic idealization of her and had noted the inequality of intellectual abilities. His critical mood had left its mark on the patient Griselda he thought Alys to be. For his part, Russell had irrational fears of her loss by disease, and he could also fantasize her as threatening him from a picture (15 November 1894); but it is Alys's uncharacteristic intuition in the midst of an ordinary exchange of letters that led her to write that she had always feared they expected too much of the relationship and would necessarily be disappointed some day (10 September 1894). The fear was not examined as it should have been, and the ideal union fatally lost cohesion, leading to great suffering before its final dissolution as late as 1921. Russell's alternating pity, contempt, and cruelty during the terminal phase of this love appear in his journal (see *Contemplation and Action, 1902–14*). The entries for 1905 are especially interesting for their scornful remarks on Alys's jealousy, an emotion which Russell was later to condemn as a needless impediment to emancipated lovemaking. He felt a genuine need for the love of women, for being cared for and caring, but he also felt apprehension about women controlling him; hence his wish to dominate preemptively in a relationship. Yet he could never merely dominate, since his need for attachment to alleviate depression was so great. Thus the obsessional managing technique he devised to keep peace with Granny distorted later relations with women—the very women who promised release from the sense of domination. He could not long tolerate intimacy, but he could not live without the assurance of being loved. As Russell wrote in a cancelled passage of the *Autobiography*, "I now believe that it is not in my nature to remain physically fond of any woman for more than seven or eight years."[3] We may anticipate from these words the series of ideal loves Russell exhibits in the correspondence, loves which are certainly with real women but are mythologized with all the romantic passion of Wagner's *Tristan und Isolde*.

The letters to Alys are brilliant apprentice work, whereas those to Lady Ottoline are art—the creations of a master writer. By his prose Russell as much creates the romance he wants as reports it. This is not to deny that the letters dig deeply into the meaning of their relationship, but they do select and heighten the ideal features of romance that Russell most desired. The letters to Ottoline reveal Russell's ultimate conflict over attachment—his imaginative escapism together with the concrete facts of being in love with a woman able to reciprocate more fully than could Alys. The confessional passages penetrate to the very core of Russell's being. When the affair began in 1911, Russell was almost thirty-nine and had achieved a considerable philosophical reputation, but he was not at peace. His turmoil demanded ministrations that could only come from a complex sufferer as strong-willed but as lonely as he. The letters to Ottoline represent a second phase of Russell's "creative illness," fuller emergence from an artificial life that had only partially been affected by the transformation of 1901. Here at last Russell reaches the ground of his divided self in search of a principle of reunion—intellect divided from feeling as Faust is divided from Don Juan. But the reunified self Russell sought had to be more than Faust and Don Juan combined: it was the universalized pacifist conscience aware of all human suffering. The most rigorous testing of his ambivalence in love was necessary before that stage could be reached.

A word about Lady Ottoline Morrell will be helpful. She is a Bloomsbury personality worthy of the closest attention, though something of an artist manqué. Mercilessly caricatured by D. H. Lawrence as Hermione Roddice in *Women in Love* and again, if with less venom, by Aldous Huxley in *Chrome Yellow*, Ottoline Morrell's life as the lady of her creation, the country house Garsington, gave cause for the occasional misunderstandings. She found it difficult to make clear to her high-powered intellectual companions exactly what she was about. Her genius proved to be for bringing about social encounters, not for the arts themselves. That Lady Ottoline was far richer in spirit and a wiser observer of people than Lawrence or Huxley could allow appears in her two volumes of *Memoirs*. Her shrewd reflections on Russell are well worth considering in connection with reports of frivolous amours. The *Memoirs* show a wise but saddened humanity quite at variance with the flamboyant stylishness Ottoline sometimes affected, and which made her vulnerable to unkind tittle-tattle. She was indeed deeply vulnerable, as her letters show—a psychosomatic sufferer who repeatedly sought supportive therapies and whose neurotic conflict sometimes ruled her life, sometimes gave it magnificence. Like Russell she was an aristocrat, a Cavendish-Bentinck, and like him she suffered parental deprivation (her father when she was four) and dislocation of life pattern. She was a woman of the deepest feeling who, schooled by the arts, developed powers of detached insight which made her Russell's most effective female companion over his long life of knowing women—with the possible exception of his last marriage. Russell learned more about himself through relations with Ottoline than in any other recorded relationship, yet the final effect seems to have stimulated not restrained, his Don Juanism. However this may be, Lady Ottoline gave back her lover aspects of himself he would not otherwise have seen.

    Russell warns Ottoline about his cold, pedantic intellect; it is folly, he says, to live by intellect alone. Full conversion to pity for suffering mankind would come by indirection, through an illusory but uplifting sensual religion of love. Long needing God (Alys's liberal Quakerism not serving), Russell gave himself fully to the modern heresy of love between man and woman as sufficient religion. The transcendent is immanent in Lady Ottoline, whose striking aristocratic beauty we know from photographs.[4] She is Russell's Beatrice or Laura; her letters are "holy presences." For each lover there is more than the thrill of an extramarital affair. Each lonely soul gains communion and enlargement by sharing experiences of nature, art, music, poetry, and philosophy. Culture of all the senses is sought and found, much beyond fleshly satisfactions. The letters vibrate with the discoveries of civilized pleasures, and at first they minimize the practical difficulties of life sustained on such a plane. Don Juan has found his paradise of aesthetic delights. The rapture of Russell's reports, as his capacity for feeling was being enlarged, must be unparalleled in modern correspondences. Readers of the *Autobiography* and of Clark's *Life* have some idea of the grandeur and incandescence of these mainly unpublished letters, but their full impact comes only when they are read as a connected sequence, with Ottoline's delightfully idiosyncratic replies.

Russell as a prose writer is surely at his best, utterly lucid as in his best philosophical writing, but in the letters to Ottoline there is a pitch of urgency that only love as revelation could bring.

> You *cannot* know how my life is changed by you—how all the good is set free, and everything else is swept out of existence. I can believe you are changed too— love is a wonderful alchemist—he turns all our baser alloys to pure gold. All the ancient splendours of the world—all its joys and heroisms and achievements—all the pity of it, the boundless sorrow and the tragedy—all that I have ever admired and lived by—all meet in my soul in one great diapason of love, love, love. O my Dearest, my Dearest, it is too divine—I feel mortal man was not meant for such joys. (#137)

Yet it is still a Russell troubled by "restless desire" who writes, one whose unmet need for attachment at last may be answered, though the reader feels doubt. It is the tension between Russell's discovery and the inherent danger of its being imperfect that gives these letters their vitality. A few quotations give the tenor of his feelings, as Lady Ottoline elicited them.

> I have so long had the superstitious feeling as being born for tragedy that it still surprises me to find happiness, and instinctively I feel that the gods must have some punishment in store for me. (#141)

> I long to lay my head on your breast and feel your soothing touch and know that even during life there is peace. . . . (#149)

I am wayward, uncertain, violent, and you are gentle with the gentleness of unconquerable strength. My whole soul worships you with utter devotion—in you it finds its home, the home it sought all the weary years. (#290)

Since my mother's miniature was destroyed I have not cared greatly for any physical object except the locket with your hair that you gave me. . . . . (#335)

It has nothing to do with physical passion—I never felt less—it is more like a child crying because its parents have left it in the dark all alone. (#513)

Beneath this is the confession, expected from the potentially depressive Russell, that only such a love as that for Lady Ottoline controls the sorrow his sense of loss gives to the human situation. His is a cosmic loneliness, almost a metaphysical principle.

Oh my love, I love you with an infinite devotion which seems to hold all the sorrow in the world within it. (#189)

Before you came into my life, recurrent anxiety was the most vivid thing in my life, and nothing was strong to put it out between times; tho' I was always trying to forget it. (#325)

I have been thinking what it is in you that holds me to you—it is chiefly, I think, the way you feel the ultimate sadness of the world—the deep tragedy of life. (#993)

Love releases from grief for loss, from loneliness and from conflict: it is his only reparative hope. "As long as all is well between you and me I feel that horror of inward discord will not come back—All these months I have had an unspeakable happiness, and a sense of regeneration and new life" (#274). A need for love so imperious, however, predicts its own instability—nothing could give Russell the ultimate sustenance he craved. Lover cannot also be mother, or not for long. The pitch of expectation was too high for safety. "I wish I were less turbulent. I feel such a boiling sea of passion I hardly know how to live with it. It is just yearning after the infinite—union with you in the infinite—I can't put it more clearly. . . ." (#431)

Russell therefore misjudged the possibility of an ideal relationship with Lady Ottoline. Though warmly responsive, her letters are never so ecstatic as his. Lady Ottoline succeeded as Russell's lay analyst during a powerful stage of emergence, but she was not to be taken from husband and daughter, nor would she alter her religious convictions. It is ironic that religion was the rock on which the relationship first split, her belief exposing his heresy. They might tolerate each other's liaisons, might accept her troublesome health, but at the deepest level her mysticism was Christian. Her unconventionality did not extend to her giving up the teaching of Mother Julian, a nun who had saved her from despair in girlhood. Irritation accumulated and in 1913 we find Russell acutely miserable in one of a series of crises that marked the affair: "I am utterly and absolutely miserable—I find I cannot face life without you—it seems so bleak and dark and terrible. . . ." (#849) Old fears of separation were aroused, but Lady Ottoline was not simply at fault.

From early in the affair Russell was aware that his love was crossed by a contrary force: the obsessional vigilance which controlled an internalized Granny, though he does not put it this way. He knew the effect but was mystified about the cause. "It is love makes me hurt you and when I love most I feel most need to hurt you—I don't know why" (#299). In the next letter he comments, "I have the furious persecutor in me—he is terribly vital. . . . I shall always be hungry for your God and blaspheming him." Russell always sought reunion after separation, but, in the wearing down of wills, revealing confessions are made: "It is so *divine* when I cease to *fear* you," he writes in 1914 (#1037). The turbulent passions of these letters are frightening. We appreciate the triumph of sublimation by which Russell the pacifist overcame violent impulses, impulses he is honest enough to convey to her. As he wrote in a difficult mood in 1915, "The search for wisdom is much more passionate in me than any earthly love, and when I feel that you are baffling me in my search it brings violent moods and a wish to tear the secret out of you by force—tho' of course *I know* that it is useless" (#1319).

Unable to convince Lady Ottoline that she should leave husband and daughter to give herself wholly to him, Russell turned to a new love. Alas, the seeds of dissolution existing in the former affair were largely present in the next. Lady Constance Malleson ("Colette") had other attachments and a strong mind of her own.

The love letters to "Colette" find Russell's conflict sharpened and simplified.[5] There are not the tortured lengthy passages of intro-spection; there are seldom the extremes of barely controlled passions; tensions of ecstasy and despair are now more clearly outlined, and the prose simpler, at times purer. The literary craftsman in Russell strove for penetrating simplicity and vividness in his appeals to this woman. Only loss of amplitude makes the letters to Colette a less remarkable "work" than the series to Ottoline. The "analysis" with Ottoline had indeed released Russell's power to feel simply and essentially. We now hear him speaking from his core to a much younger woman who yet understood his loneliness and despair—replying from her own similar positions but in a lighter, less knowing and world-weary vein than had Lady Ottoline. Colette's was a remarkable spirit, capable of fresh perceptions and of a new kind of love.

In *After Ten Years: A Personal Record*, Constance Malleson (who preferred the stage name Colette O'Niel) explains her parentage and early life. She was of the Northern Irish aristocracy, growing up at Castlewellan, a house and garden of great beauty in the Mountains of Mourne. In her youth she also did the London season. Colette's father was a peer, thirty-five years older than her vivacious Dublin socialite mother, his second wife and a cousin. In her autobiography Colette allows that he could be remote and gloomy, on occasion tyrannical; but she had "an unexpressed and greatly daring love for him" that resisted the imputation of Castlewellan womenfolk that her father was an ogre. Her closest attachment was, nevertheless, to an English nurse, neither parent quite satisfactory as a model. Independence and loneliness, but an inquiring spirit and a hunger for emancipated action, characterize Colette's self-portrayal. She set out on a brief and only moderately successful acting career, her gifts being perhaps more fully realized as a novelist and autobiographer. She had a gift for portraying the life she lived in London and later as a traveller and resident in Scandinavia. In *The Coming Back* she fictionalizes at a reflective distance her relations with Russell, bringing in Lady Otto-line and others of that older set. Colette tries, if only with limited success, to take the measure of this fascinating but maddening man of genius. She remained loyal until her death in 1975 to her ideal Russell, an ideal only somewhat resembling the man she never entirely knew, despite more than fifty years of exchanges. The best of them come early.

These are letters of war years, the relationship beginning in 1916 by their pacifist No-Conscription Fellowship connection. "In a world of hate, she preserved love, love in every sense of the word from the most ordinary to the most profound, and she had a quality of rock-like immovability," Russell wrote of Colette.[6] She was certainly more complicated than this suggests, yet Colette brought Russell solace and renewal in the years that most acutely tested his pacifism by imprisonment. In the Edwardian heyday of Ottoline, it was hardly predictable that such a time of proving one's principles lay ahead. Pacifism, we have seen, grew from Russell's perception of the mystery of sadness at the heart of every human life. Psychologically it was a fortunate reaction-formation against his own violent impulses, by which they were civilized in accord with what he felt about suffering. Colette too felt the sadness of loss and despair over loss, and she complemented Russell's desire to reach beyond the anguish of Europe torn by military strife. Lady Ottoline by this time was immersed in caring for conscientious objectors at Garsington and could not give Russell the intimacy he required. (The correspondence with her, however, continued until her death in 1938.) Again an idyll of perfected, redeeming love was attempted, yet with Colette also the moments of ecstasy were invaded by practical difficulties and contrary emotions which denied the peace he wished. Don Juan suffered by craving yet fearing attachment, by fearing while risking loss of love.

Striving to transcend the limitations of circumstances, Russell writes that he feels profoundly a need of something she alone has to give, that can only come of freedom away together (2 March 1917). He feels full of life struggling up into being (26 October 1916), due to erotic passion for her youthful charms; but also, he eventually admits, the urgent attachment to her is due to feeling like a child in the dark needing protection (16 April 1918). These wartime letters often find Russell at his most insecure and pessimistic. The only consolation is love. His love is sometimes as hot and raging as a forest fire, but sometimes as gentle as a spring shower kissing the timid flowers (21 September 1917). The world, Russell says, lives by a great desire—a reaching out after something unknown. This is his constant plea: that there is some great good to be had but which just eludes him. He begs Colette to love him or he must perish; without her he is nothing, an empty shell, but with her he is a god. Hers was the stimulation he craved, a stimulation of mind and body, even to the point of grandiose wishes (21 September 1917). But talk of love-religion is less flagrant in these letters. It is replaced by a theme more fundamental: the need for maternal comfort and reassurance, a sort of second beginning for infancy-starved Russell. He poignantly complains of being tortured and miserable, hoping to find rest lying in her arms. He asks if she will allow him to creep into her arms and lie very still, like a baby. Will she show mercy to a poor wounded suffering thing, he asks. He does not ask for passion but to come home (2 November 1917). This reminds us of his earlier fruitless search for "the beautiful vision—God," a search which became a "passionate love for a ghost"—the ghost of lost attachments to parents and the probable origin of Russell's depressive compassion for humanity.[7] Without his ghosts he would have been no pacifist, but a cynical Don Juan indeed. The unrealized infant in himself, insofar as Russell remained in touch, was less an embarrassment than a source of moral strength.

What led to the collapse of the relationship with Colette, or rather to its repeated collapses and revivals? Russell could not help but be Colette's mentor, encouraging and admonishing her through the struggle to begin a stage career and to write. But he tried also to act as her conscience, criticizing her vanity and lack of control over impulses. She lacked in social responsibility, he said, and at times he found her lacking in human understanding. Having left her husband, Miles Malleson, her liaison with yet another man, "Maurice," troubled Russell, despite agreement that they should be free. His benevolent but frustrated tie to T. S. Eliot's first wife complicated matters, but beneath this was the old ambivalence about women, the double feeling of hunger and resentment, aggravated by Colette's similar attitude toward men. This leaves the correspondence as torn by contraries as that to Lady Ottoline. Not only had Russell the methodical work side, and the wildly passionate, possessive side, but the passionate side was itself divided into passive and active, helping and hurting impulses (4 January 1918). As he was forced to confess to her, his life was poisoned by pain, and it was hell for everyone to come very close to him (14 January 1918). Earlier he had written that he had spread pain everywhere because of a ruthless and insatiable devouring hunger (25 October 1917). Yet Russell and his "heart's comrade" never quite parted, remaining in touch even in old age, neither fully able to share the enclosed and separate pain each felt. The records of this remarkable relationship are very full, and one day, when publication becomes possible, we will have a panorama of it. These letters, like the correspondence with Lady Ottoline, make a literary work in their own right.

Some conclusions appear from this sampling of three of Russell's love correspondences. First, Russell became a consummate letter writer, emulating the great nineteenth-century correspondences, such as that of Thomas and Jane Welsh Carlyle. But more than they he shapes and heightens as a fiction writer would, and he is self-critically analytical where earlier letter writers were content to be gently evocative and descriptive. Russell was a natural autobiographer, attuned to every spiritual advance and setback, which he phrased for effect as a truth-seeking seventeenth-century Puritan would do. At the same time Russell was a moralist in a new exploratory vein, a "liberator" of pent-up passions or, more accurately, one willing to state the strength of desire for passionate attachment. His affairs raised eyebrows; his opinions caused scandals; early his aunt Agatha berated him for "misconduct with women—married women. . . . Promiscuous connections I hate."[8] Later in America he was stigmatized by a Jesuit publication as a "desiccated, divorced, and decadent advocate of sexual promiscuity. . . ."[9] Don Juan suits him, but with qualification. Russell's was an obsessional personality all right, as was D. H. Lawrence's and John Middleton Murry's. Like them his tumultuous emotions sometimes hurt innocent persons and brought hurt upon himself.

But Russell had a larger measure of the tragic sense than had most of the pacifist and socialist allies: he saw beyond what they saw into the heart of human sadness, never forgetting that all life hangs by a thread and that its severing can be quite arbitrary. Grandmother seems to have implanted lasting resentment of women, leading to Russell's controlling obsessionality, but she also left a strong ancestral sense of moral and social duty. It was this that empowered Russell to speak out fearlessly against all cruelty and senseless contention, as he did most eloquently during the antinuclear weapons campaign of the late 1950s and early 1960s. He triumphed morally by rising above the warring contraries in himself to denounce all preparation for war and to speak on behalf of a rededicated humanity. "Remember your humanity and forget the rest" was his message: fine words, but dare we credit them from someone who had so little peace in himself? Without his personal struggle for love, it is doubtful that Russell could have recognized how lethal but, alternatively, how majestic, human passions can be. He lived its full range of destructive and constructive possibilities.

But did Russell remember all the shades of compromise to which humanity resorts? When nuclear weapons were not renounced by the world powers and balance of terror became a way of life, disillusioned followers turned from the bright vision of a warless world to the self-indulgent sexual "liberation" that Russell had long seemed to advocate. "Make love not war" became the catchword. Much more soberly, Russell had written as early as 1929, "There can be no doubt that to close one's mind on marriage against all the approaches of love from elsewhere is to diminish receptivity and sympathy and the opportunities of valuable human contacts."[10] How intellectualized this is compared to the immediate protestations of his letters, but it is saying the same thing for public consumption. "Liberation" came with a public display completely unlike Russell's own style, which was fastidiously aristocratic. He did not set out to shock but to satisfy an unappeasable hunger, a need to be mothered much after the time had passed. The liberated generation did not bother to examine the real meaning of Russell's experience of ecstatic but disruptive and, too often, unfulfilling love. They ignored, or failed to see, what even the *Autobiography* discloses as reasons for so arduous a love quest. We may not be biologically monogamous (as the psychobiologists are saying), but at least we find monogamy socially most advantageous for the purpose of raising children. Russell never faced the question whether

Don Juanism can be compatible with social cohesion and the rights of children. He suggested no means of containing the promiscuity he helped sanction, perhaps because he could not foresee the magnitude and complexity of the present-day interpersonal problems "permissiveness" has brought. It is, of course, unfair to lay blame for our present confusion at Russell's doorstep, but if any mind could have penetrated it, had he looked ahead and been moved to do so, his could. Surely Russell would have said that the sexual freedoms of the late twentieth century are as dangerous as was Victorian repressiveness. In order for us better to understand his situational morality, a much more sensitive account than has yet been given of Russell's loss and attempted symbolic repair needs to be given.

The complicated genesis of Russell's campaign to change conventional views of sexuality, and of that to change conventional views of conflict, needs to be dealt with separately.

Notes

1. Alistair Cooke, *Six Men* (New York: Knopf, 1977), p. 177.
2. Russell, "Our Women Haters," *Mortals and Others: Bertrand Russell's American Essays 1931–1935*, ed. Harry Ruja (London: George Allen & Unwin, 1975), p. 90.
3. Quoted in Ronald W. Clark, *The Life of Bertrand Russell* (London: Cape and Weidenfeld and Nicolson, 1975), p. 88.
4. See Carolyn G. Heilbrun (ed.), *Lady Ottoline's Album* (London: Michael Joseph, 1976).
5. These letters, on deposit together with replies in the Bertrand Russell Archives at McMaster University, may not be quoted until the entire correspondence is published. Those cited were paraphrased.
6. Russell, *Autobiography* II, p. 26.
7. Ibid., p. 75.
8. Quoted in Clark, pp. 326–27.
9. Quoted in Clark, p. 470.
10. Russell, *Marriage and Morals*, p. 113.

CHAPTER

7

The Angry Pacifist

I long to alleviate the evil, but I cannot, and I too suffer.
—Russell, "What I Have Lived For"

Reflection on Bertrand Russell's biography raises the question whether he was indeed the pacifist he claimed to be. Unrealistic sainthood can be asked of any pacifist, but in Russell's case there are indications that he was no pacifist at all while maintaining the stance of one. I refer to the discrepancy between the public profession of pacifism, beginning with the First World War, and private fantasy and behavior. Can Russell's politics of pacifism be faulted for having been at variance with his own violent urges, or is there a principle by which his pacifism can be authenticated? From the Boer War to Vietnam Russell was consistently sensitive to the suffering caused by war; only now with accumulated biographical evidence can we begin to explain how this tormented man became one of the twentieth century's most effective advocates of peace. It is important to speculate about how his grief and rage were converted into socially useful forms yet left evidence of their source in psychological conflict.

So far historians lack the concepts to describe Russell's attitude to war. In her study of Russell's part in the No Conscription Fellowship during the Great War, Jo Vellacott finds insufficient "evidence of a positively pacifist outlook" developing between his "conversion" of 1901 and the outbreak of war in 1914.[1] She recognizes Russell's own violent streak, and notes the tendency through the experience of war "towards an integration of the different sides of personality"; but there is no theory to explain what occurred.[2] Thomas C. Kennedy writes more bluntly that Russell was "never a pacifist," because his stance was less due to personal faith than it was to a political strategy.[3] Let us see whether psychobiography helps to clear up this matter.

The Great War drew from Russell some of his most urgent statements about the need to control hostility in its collective form. He reacted with horror to the killing in what Henry James called "the plunge of civilization into this abyss of blood and darkness."[4] In "Why Nations Love War" (1914) Russell saw in public zest for armed conflict the most serious obstacle to pacifism, and he outlined the psychological issue. The same people who deplored the evil of war seemed to enjoy it, the result of "an instinctive disposition of human nature," "the instinct of every gregarious animal to cooperate with members of its own herd and to oppose members of other herds."[5] He also discussed the needs of urban people for excitement, the lust for power and fear of domination by an enemy, along with the appealing selflessness of military service. Each reason for war is hard for the pacifist to answer, but Russell proposed, as William James had done, a moral alternative to war in which instinctive hostility is deconditioned by using appropriate stimuli, with sport serving as a substitute for lethal contests. Thus Russell turned to psychology to address the problem of removing war, but the war continued and he pressed for moral ways to resist its ravages. In "The Philosophy of Pacifism" (1915) he advocated passive resistance which "would discourage the use of force by arousing a sense of shame in the aggressive nation, and also by the fact that it would be found able to preserve whatever is worth preserving in the life of the nation which had the courage to employ it."[6] Russell was never an absolute pacifist: in "War and Non-Resistance" (1915) he made clear that he did not favor the views of the Quakers and Tolstoy that "it is always wrong to employ force against another human being." But he advocated limiting the use of force and questioned the justifiability of armed self-defense. Only force within a neutral rule of law as "in a central government of the world" should be sanctioned.[7] These are surely the opinions of a sensitive, responsible, and far-seeing thinker shocked by modern war into finding its remedy. Yet it was wittily remarked by A. E. Housman that "If I were the Prince of Peace, I would choose a less provocative Ambassador," so aggressive was Russell about his anti-war opinions.[8] As is well known, he was dismissed in 1916 from his lectureship at

Trinity College, Cambridge, having been found guilty under the Defence of the Realm Act for his part in the "Everett Leaflet," which supported the rights of conscientious objection. In 1918 he went to prison for six months for having published further remarks about the war "likely to prejudice His Majesty's relations with the United States of America."[9]

Russell was a more or less militant pacifist from that time on. During the 1920s and 30s his popular essays frequently refer to the danger of another European war. For instance, in 1924 he wrote: "Those of us who do not wish to see our whole civilization go down in red ruin have a great and difficult duty to perform—to guard the door of our minds against patriotism."[10] But by 1939 he was convinced that the Nazi tyranny had to be resisted by force: "I remained in favour of peace until shortly before the outbreak of the Second World War when I became convinced that peace with Hitler was impossible."[11] Even through that struggle Russell thought of himself as "still a pacifist in the sense that I think peace the most important thing in the world."[12] With the rise of East-West tensions, Russell became a nuclear disarmer willing to use civil disobedience to put before the public the vastly increased dangers of war fought with nuclear weapons. As he said in "Man's Peril" (1955), "Shall we put an end to the human race; or shall mankind renounce war?"[13] At the end of his life he opposed the American presence in Vietnam, and insured that his opposition to war would outlive him by setting up a Peace Foundation.

II.

Following the exhilaration felt on completion of a draft of *The Principles of Mathematics*, Russell was plunged "into the darkest despair that I have ever known," caused by intellectual and emotional problems compounding each other (*Autobiography* I, 145). This despair was brought dramatically to an end with the mystic illumination of 1901, to which Russell attributed his pacifism. In his discussion of conversion in *The Varieties of Religious Experience* William James refers to "subconsciously maturing processes."[14] In Ellenberger's terms, as we have seen, this is the "creative illness" in which unconscious cerebration leads to a sudden psychological or moral discovery of lasting value. It is well to repeat Russell's report of his insight:

> Within five minutes I went through some such reflections as the following: the loneliness of the human soul is unendurable; nothing can penetrate it except the highest intensity of the sort of love that religious teachers have preached; whatever does not spring from this motive is harmful, or at best useless; it follows that war is wrong . . . that the use of force is to be deprecated, and that in human relations one should penetrate to the core of loneliness in each person and speak to that. (I, 146)

Russell claims that the conversion made him "a completely different person," no longer concerned "only for exactness and analysis" but caring for beauty and for the lives of others (I, 146). It was an "emotional set-back" but with enormous potential for his future as a social critic (I, 147). The term "pacifist" is used to describe his new state of mind. There followed "an intense interest in children, and . . . a desire almost as profound as that of the Buddha to find some philosophy which should make human life endurable."

Having re-experienced, through the medium of the Whitehead's three-year-old son, his anxiety at the time of loss of his own parents, Russell was forced to alter his view of life's meaning to one of tragedy and suffering. As he put it in "The Return to the Cave": "We are orphans and exiles, lost children wandering in the night."[15] But feelings of radical separation must be sublimated if we are to endure: "So out of pity grows service, out of service grows love, and out of love grows wisdom and the power of endurance," as he wrote in an untitled paragraph of *The Pilgrimage of Life*.[16] Russell's new world picture is most eloquently presented in "The Free Man's Worship" (1903), where he argues that while the universe seems to care nothing for our struggles, we must learn to care about our fellow men by acquiring the tragic view of life:

> In the spectacle of Death, in the endurance of intolerable pain, and in the irrevocableness of a vanished past, there is a sacredness . . . in which . . . the sufferer is bound to the world by bonds of sorrow.[17]

Russell came to dislike such lyric language, but he never disavowed its message that because lonely suffering is the tragic law of life, we should not increase the suffering of our fellow human beings. This became the foundation of his politics of pacifism and, however much he altered his ethical theorizing and adjusted pacifist principles to political realities, the conversion always remained a major reference point.

I have suggested that Russell's acquiring a tragic view of life, what he called the "religion of sorrow," was a product of a "creative illness." While the term leaves something to be desired, it connotes a process of long incubation or moral unrest, leading to a discovery of a universal application benefitting humanity. The discovery is invariably surrounded by repressed infant and childhood conflicts which at last are organized into a vision of how social good may be promoted. The moment of reorganization is precipitated by relaxation after intense intellectual effort, when subcurrents of obsessional thinking surface and form meaning. A new stage of moral growth is initiated, with matters too private for words being "converted" into an urge for public reforms. For Russell the conversion of 1901 released him from regressive longings for refuge in pure Platonic essences, from Pythagorean mysticism of number, into a new politics of human concern. The first result was to renounce British imperialism and become pro-Boer. Consistently thereafter, with each new armed conflict, Russell saw it for the suffering it caused, not just for its political rights and wrongs.

But can so large an effect as his lifelong pacifism be attributed to a brief five-minute "conversion," and what of the credibility of his statement that "I had become a *completely* different person" (my italics)? People are reluctant to accept as genuine such claims to instant and complete moral change. (This is not just because "conversion" is now rare among intellectuals—it implies a prior condition of radical disjunction between thought and affect, common among such Victorians as John Stuart Mill and Havelock Ellis who are known to have had secular conversions. Russell the logician had indeed been an affectless "thinking machine" who found release from Victorian inhibitions.) Doubts arise because of Russell's stormy personal life revealed in the *Autobiography*, examined by the biographer Ronald Clark (1975) and lavishly documented in Russell's still mainly unpublished private correspondence. With all that is known of Russell's complicated affairs with women, with four marriages and three divorces, it is impossible to see him as a modern "saint." So tormented are his feelings about women that it is unlikely that his popular writings on marriage and sexual morality will ever again be read purely for their "ideas." Russell the sexual freedom fighter reveals, especially in the letters he left to posterity, the intense interpersonal conflicts which wounded many of the women with whom he had begun the most "ideal" of relationships. Feminists point to the case of Helen Dudley, whom Russell lured from America back to Britain only to abandon, which contributed, he allows, to her later insanity (I, 213–14). The "conversion" which enjoined him to "penetrate to the core of loneliness in each person and speak to that" therefore looks suspect in the light of his promiscuous sexual strivings, with their implicit aggression.

World War I only accentuated his antagonism to Puritan repressiveness, which he thought had led to venting the rage which made war. Anticipating the slogan "make love not war," he wrote "that only through the diffusion of instinctive joy can a good world be brought into being" (II, 39), an evidence of the uncritical Freudianism he had been introduced to about this time. In 1916 Russell began one of his most serious affairs, that with Lady Constance Malleson. In this adventure with a younger woman he pressed further the liberation of the senses begun in his affair with Lady Ottoline Morrell, the inspired hostess of Bloomsbury fame. Pacifism in wartime made him feel both more an outsider in a jingoistic society and more boldly idealistic about how society should be reorganized for a warless world, especially through early education. Writing at his most Lawrentian in the preface to *Principles of Social Reconstruction*, Russell said, "I consider the best life that which is most built on creative impulses, and the worst that which is most inspired by love of possession."[18] It all sounds naive, even unconsciously duplicitous, when possessiveness is thought of in terms of the sexual jealousies Russell believed need not hamper his urges.

To what extent was Russell the victim of his own confusion about love and violence? In the light of his sexual aggressiveness, and other more intellectual forms of anger, should the conversion be seen as mainly specious? It is in the conjunction of grief and rage, reactive to developmental factors, that I believe Russell's importance as a "pacifist" lies. However fast the conversion faded, it seems to have been an authentic reparative closure of Russell's split ego, a healing vision of pity for human suffering and his most powerful instruction to give care. That contrary psychological factors, unrealized by Russell, prevented carrying through his design to relieve human loneliness and to renounce the use of force should not disqualify the intention. (Russell never sought analysis, relying mainly on what he could piece together for himself and confide by letter to his women in a sort of autoanalysis.) The reasons he gave for the conversion therefore seem not to have been the only or even the main ones. Let us look at the violent trend in Russell's personality.

III

At the end of his life an admirer described Russell as "gentle, shy, modest, even vulnerable. Cruelty he hated, and he felt deeply the pains of others. He himself radiated that 'kindly feeling' which he held to be the hope of the world."[19] But recollections of earlier encounters show something different. Sidney Hook points to "a strong streak of cruelty": Russell "would often and needlessly deliver himself of the most devastating things about some individuals, and enjoy it," as Hook remembers from his days in New York in the 1940s.[20] These were difficult times for Russell, but even after the conversion, Russell had showed hostility of an intensity not usual in pacifists. In 1903, when his reputation as a logician was established, Russell enjoyed showing his powers: John Maynard Keynes reported of an evening gathering that "for hours on Saturday night Russell wiped the floor with a man called Leonard Hobhouse—a most superb display."[21] In a depressive fantasy Russell could do worse than this. Writing to Gilbert Murray (whose poetic reading had moved Russell to his conversion) he confessed:

> I have been merely oppressed by the weariness and tedium and vanity of things lately: nothing stirs me, nothing seems worth doing or worth having done: the only thing that I strongly *feel* worth while would be to murder as many people as possible so as to diminish the amount of consciousness in the world. These times have to be lived through: there is nothing to be done with them.[22]

The *Autobiography* gives evidence that Russell had difficulty controlling his violent impulses. Speaking of an adolescent friend called Fitzgerald, Russell says:

> I came to hate him with a violence which, in retrospect, I can hardly understand. On one occasion, in an excess of fury, I got my hands on his throat and started to strangle him. I intended to kill him, but when he began to grow livid, I relented. I do not think he knew that I had intended murder. (I, 44)

Commenting on the anxieties that surrounded his first marriage in 1894 to Alys Pearsall Smith, Russell reviewed the "tragedies" in his family which made procreation seem dangerous.

> The fears generated . . . have never ceased to trouble me subconsciously. Ever since, but not before, I have been subject to violent nightmares in which I dream that I am being murdered, usually by a lunatic. I scream out loud, and on one occasion, before waking, I nearly strangled my wife, thinking that I was defending myself against a murderous assault. (I, 85–86)

More than a reminiscence of a disordered uncle who had committed such a murder (I, 31), this event suggests repressed hostility to women. The impression is supported by a later remark:

> I remember . . . a day after three weeks of marriage, when, under the influence of sexual fatigue, I hated her and could not imagine why I had wished to marry her. (I, 124)

The marriage gradually lapsed with Alys becoming depressed at her husband's unresponsiveness and rejection. The journal Russell kept from 1902 to 1905 is a moral balance sheet in which pity for her vies with his mounting dislike of all her ways. He sees, yet deplores, the possibility of escape "into more or less flirtatious relations with women I don't respect."[23] Both hope of erotic deliverance and mistrust of women appear in this statement.

The strength of Russell's ambivalence about love and hate is evident in confessional letters to Lady Ottoline Morrell. In 1911 she had induced what Russell called a second conversion, enlarging his sensibility after the ascetic controls that had permitted the writing of *Principia Mathematica*. In Lady Ottoline, Russell found a woman to whom he could impart the tumult of his desires and aversions; he appealed to her to witness his inner violence, and yet eventually she too lost his confidence and was replaced.

> I think sometimes you think it is only peccadillos I am afraid of, but it isn't; it is the big violent crimes—murder and suicide and such things. I don't know what is the right way to deal with this violence in me—I know it is bad, but it is bound up with good things so intimately that it is hard to disentangle.[24]

Russell was trying to work through with her his obsessive-compulsive violence and make real the cleansing purity of perfect love. Writing to her in Paris the next day, he complains of the separation and cautions her against "praising Desire again": it is a "fierce fiend" and "very near to cruelty," as though erotic love were some sort of punishment he had to hand out to his women. Then follows one of the most alarming confessions made anywhere in the letters, but one also showing insight and the protective function of reason:

> I do wish I could get inside your skin and know what it feels like to be you. Sometimes I think I know, and sometimes I think I don't. I doubt if even you know how nearly I am a raving madman. Of all the characters I ever read about in fiction, none was so intimate to me as Raskolnikov. It is only intellect that keeps me sane; perhaps this makes me overvalue intellect as against feeling. I remember when I wanted to commit murder, the beginning was a sudden picture (I hardly have pictures at ordinary times) of a certain way of doing it, quite vivid, with the act visible before my eyes; it lived with me then for ever so long, always haunting me; I took to reading about murders and thinking about them, and always with that picture before me. It was only hard thinking that kept me straight at that time—the impulse was not amenable to morals, but it was amenable to reasoning that this was madness.[25]

That Russell occasionally suffered from what seem like thought disturbances, from flights into science fiction-like fantasies of destruction, appears in a letter to Lady Ottoline of the next year in which he speaks of the "fanatic" being in conflict with the "lover."

> Vast visions haunt me—I see the whole human race ringed about with fire, in a vast alchemist's crucible that produces a few quintessential

> jewels from the ashes of the holocaust. I know this is madness . . .
> melodramatic rubbish—but although my intellect tells me it is absurd,
> I still go on feeling the same way. My love for you gets entangled in this
> world of delirium. . . .[26]

A certain amount of self-dramatization appears in these letters, but
mainly they should be taken as true portrayals of the lover's states
swinging between ecstasy and sometimes suicidal wishes, with stabili-
zations always being sought and sanity a constant quest. An instance
of the struggle for consistency of purpose is suggested by the following
remarks to Lady Ottoline:

> I have been too fierce, too violent, too destructive—something of the
> cruelty of the ascetic has been in me—but Dearest these things will
> melt away. . . .
>
> I am filled with utter love and longing for service—to bring happiness,
> to bring relief from pain—oh if I could. I hate the furious persecutor in
> me—but he is terribly vital. I try to be kind in a common way—yet I do
> strangely little for others.[27]

Russell's self-monitoring love letters are the confessions of a continuing "creative illness" in which the discovery of humanistic pacifism
remained on trial. The precariousness of his pacifism became apparent to the more astute observers. D. H. Lawrence, with whom Russell
had a brief and catastrophic intellectual relationship when they both
rebelled against the barbarity of World War I, saw the angry "fanatic" in Russell more clearly than did any of his co-workers in the peace
movement. Russell candidly reports in his *Autobiography* Lawrence's
remarks which at the time had devastated him:

> When I objected to war because of the suffering that it causes, he
> accused me of hypocrisy. "It isn't in the least true that you, your basic
> self, want ultimate peace. You are satisfying in an indirect, false way
> your lust to jab and strike. Either satisfy it in a direct and honourable
> way, saying 'I hate you all, liars and swine, and am out to set upon
> you,' or stick to mathematics, where you can be true—But to come as
> the angel of peace—no, I prefer Tirpitz a thousand times in that role."
> (II, 22)

To remark on Lawrence's own unappeasable anger is not to deny truth to his insight. But the observation is only partially accurate, and it fails to account for Russell's mentality being quite different from the warrior's, which sees reality only in power relations. The conversion went a long way toward controlling the rage of which Russell had reason to be afraid; an empathizing tragic sense suffused his view of politics, making him a highly unusual figure in our century of violence.

IV

I believe that Bennett and Nancy Simon are correct to associate Russell's pacifism with contacting in the conversion his repressed grief for loss of parents; however, they mistake the main source of his aggressiveness. They also miss much of the detail of his struggle for its containment. Russell's feelings about afflicted women, especially mothers such as Mrs. Whitehead, were not all pitying identification —though of course identification can be a hostility-reducing defense. Russell was indeed compelled by women's suffering, but, as noted, he felt strong ambivalence, even outright hostility, when his idealizations of them were unsettled. The love letters sometimes find him making mothers of lovers only to decide that the woman is coming too dangerously close. The Simons say that aggression is connected with object loss, thinking of the frustration of a seeming abandonment and the guilt carried from the three-year-old who might have thought he caused the deaths of his parents. There is some truth in this—early separations do cause protest, before causing despair and detachment in the absence of adequate substitute caregiving. But the actual dynamics are speculative.[28]

It is certain, however, that great frustration and rage were engendered in Russell's relations with his principal substitute parent, his grandmother who took him in about age four at Pembroke Lodge. Of Lady John Russell, the Simons say only that she was "peculiar" and sexually repressive, though she had advanced anti-imperialist opinions, among other strong views, which must have influenced Russell. To analyze the complicated character of this gifted aristocratic woman would take an essay in itself; the biography by her daughter and Desmond MacCarthy is too adulatory to catch her power to control others along with the love she inspired. She appears to have been what Matthew Besdine calls a "Jocasta Mother," who, in the absence of a fulfilling love life of her own, focuses affect hunger on the child. The result is a "fused symbiosis, with no effective father to help in the child's separation, self-differentiation and growth towards maturing autonomy and identity."[29] Elsewhere Besdine writes, "as the Jocasta mother continues the symbiosis on into the Oedipal period and beyond, the child, young adult and adult, experiences love and intimacy as a contaminated, incestuous, guilty bondage. It forever undermines his human relationships."[30] He gives a profile of this type of personality, a constellation which, to some extent, describes Russell, though of course he had a modicum of male influence from elder brother and uncle.

> Such Jocasta-reared children have a definite character structure marked by an unresolved Oedipus problem, the fear of love, strong ambivalence in human relations, strong paranoid trends, a tenuous ability to conform or accept authority, an underlying sense of guilt and masochism, a strong homosexual component, latent or overt, and high ambitions. . . . He is usually above average intellectually, may have unusual gifts and talents and frequently provides the leadership in rebellious movements. It is the personality found most frequently in geniuses and extraordinary achievers.[31]

Not all of these attributes might apply, and each needs careful discussion and qualification. The main issue here is the frustration-caused aggression of a degree of Jocasta mothering and how Russell dealt with it constructively by becoming a pacifist instead of an angry demagogue.

The conversion helped to release Russell from bondage to his grandmother's internalized wishes that he become great in her way. She had a masculine side, ambitious for political achievement, though she was also an unworldly Victorian moralist with strong religious preoccupations. Russell's conversion established moral imperatives of his own, relieving his almost schizoid sense of isolation which led him toward mysticism rather than to her evangelicalism. By means of the conversion he contacted the feminine, caring part of himself—the residue of his caring mother, who had also been a social reformer. His social purpose thus organized itself around a deeper center of grief and compassion for loss. It may further be conjectured that the conversion validated a reaction formation against his frustration and rage with the Jocasta over-control of his grandmother's many years of close supervision. When it is unseemly to express resentment against such a parent substitute, a more devious course is followed, reversing resentment into profession of love. Reaction formation is a well-known defensive concomitant of the obsessional personality. In the *Autobiography* Russell's grandmother's portrait is astringently written(I, 20f) compared to the brief, glowing sketch of his dead mother as "vigorous, lively, witty, serious, original, and fearless" as well as being "beautiful" (I, 15). (His father is less flatteringly remembered.) Clearly the ideal past had more appeal than recollections of his actual upbringing. Not surprisingly it was always the *ideal* lover Russell sought and remained with until the problem of intimacy and commitment arose, at which point she ceased to be ideal. Ambivalence toward women was thus doubly involved in the turn toward "peace" in 1901. Pain and pity over loss of parents, particularly the idealized mother, sensitized him to all human suffering, while an insecure reaction formation toward his grandmother empowered the destructive side of his romantic and erotic relations with women.

This is a point raised by the psychoanalyst Harry Guntrip in "Sigmund Freud and Bertrand Russell." Impressed by Russell's conversion insight into schizoid loneliness, Guntrip argues that if Russell had been able to build theoretically on this insight, he could have been a greater theorist than Freud, who got only to the level of Oedipal analysis. However, Guntrip is misled in thinking that Russell's wife Alys had been mainly a "protective bulwark" against his schizoid loneliness, and that, with the conversion, "quite suddenly the secret schizoid isolated core of him, which could neither love nor relate, erupted and destroyed his marriage."[32] Each of his loves in turn was such a "protective bulwark" so long as he could identify her with the idealized lost and unremembered mother. When intimacy and the humdrum of daily life rubbed the gilt off this image, she became identified not only with the abandoning mother but with a loving yet over-controlling grandmother from whom he wanted to escape. This was not a function of the conversion, which merely made conscious a process of recognizing sorrow over loss and began its integration into his world view.

Russell's empathy in the conversion was not solely with Mrs.

Whitehead. She was isolated, "cut off from everyone and everything by walls of agony . . ." (I, 146), while he identified with her three-year-old son whom he led away—thereby forming a lasting bond as a sort of suffering double. (Significantly for Russell's reconstruction in the *Autobiography*, the boy was a casualty of war in 1918.) The vignette of a child witnessing the agony and possible death of his mother forced upon Russell an acknowledgment of his own vulnerability and a welling up of empathetic grief. The "loneliness of the human soul" indeed felt "unendurable" to one whose mourning for his dead parents seems to have been incomplete (I, 146).

As a post-Freudian interested in the therapy of schizoid states, Guntrip is rightly impressed by Russell's insight, but he overstates the case in attributing the sudden rejection of Alys to it. Barbara Strachey Halpern clarifies by saying that Russell's emerging revulsion against Alys and her family was reflected in Alys's despair of November 1901, and that "by January Bertie was aware that his love for Alys was dying."[33] The sudden conversion of 10 February 1901 indeed resembles his later sudden realization that he no longer loved Alys, but they are not causally linked. While Russell claims that "I had no idea until this moment that my love for her was even lessening," it is fair to say that the feelings had been long incubating although Russell was reluctant to admit that his unconventional and hard-bought marriage was about to crumble. Halpern writes, "clearly his claim of total ignorance was unjustified."[34] It seems that rather than a schizoid eruption destroying his marriage, there was a breakthrough of hostility to controlling women which builds up in the Jocasta-reared male—a point which, if Guntrip had had the biographical evidence before him, he would undoubtedly have reconsidered.

Unable to accept the full strength of his angry feelings toward controlling women, Russell "converted" them into the conviction that "the use of force is to be deprecated," the pacifist credo which is a problematic stance in the politics of the "real world." It is little wonder that Russell's pacifist love of humanity always had a lofty generality about it, and that he was often at odds with himself as to how to make applications. (The most notorious instance was his equivocation over advocacy at the end of World War II of threatening a nuclear strike against the U.S.S.R. to prevent an arm race.[35]) It is difficult to connect the microcosm of childhood feelings with policies and actions later adopted by so public a figure as Russell. Yet without such attempts there is little chance of understanding how, for instance, he could so strongly advocate women's suffrage from about 1906—standing as a suffrage candidate in the election of 1907—and yet be so cruel in his alienation from Alys who was also active in social reform. Nor is it otherwise easy to see how Russell's idealizing amours were tied into his compulsion to advocate peace in the midst of war.

To some extent Russell knew what he was up against in managing his own anger. He certainly must have been thinking about it when in 1919 he wrote "On 'Bad Passions'," a paper on "the treatment of impulses recognized as undesirable, such as anger, cruelty, envy, etc." Russell argues that simple thwarting will not control these passions, which are apt "to break out with a violence all the greater owing to repression." Following the Freudian Stanley Hall, Russell agrees that much good work is actually fueled by anger, but that this is undesirable. Anger needs to be socially controlled by rewards and punishments, but most of the discussion is of intellectual and artistic sublimations of rage, a "tigerish fury" which otherwise "would have to vent itself on human beings."[36] While Russell advocates sublimation, he knows that the most creative personalities, such as Beethoven's, are always in some degree oppressive to others. He could be speaking for himself, and here there is at least a delineation of his own dynamic set in a moral framework.

Russell's own writings show him to have been examining psychological mechanisms related to reaction formation as having sociopolitical applications. As early as "Gentleness" in *The Pilgrimage of Life* (c. 1902) he wrote that as "each separate person . . . is an end in himself," power relations must be renounced, but that this is difficult.[37] In *Power: A New Social Analysis* (1938) he argues that "the tendency to cruel forms of idealism is increased by unhappiness in childhood, and would be lessened if early education were emotionally what it ought to be."[38] Many popular essays direct remarks to reforming early education in ways that reduce the strivings to implement hidden aggression by grasping for power. Several essays have shrewd psychological analyses exactly on the points which troubled him most. In "Leisure and Mechanism" (1923) he wrote, "a great deal of morality is a cloak for hostility posing as 'true kindness,' and enabling the virtuous to think that in persecuting others out of their 'vices' they are conferring a benefit."[39] By 1928 he was unmasking the pretentions of power-seeking: "very many people, and among them a majority of those who achieve positions of eminence, have deep down in their unconscious a kind of rage and hatred against the world for something it has refused them."[40] By this time Russell was well read in the psychologies of Freud and the behaviorist John B. Watson, by whose theories he sought to understand the perceptible drift toward another world war. Rage was seen as an outcome of fear, and, unable to find its true object, it tyrannizes over those who appear weak. "Ungovernable rage is a psychological aberration, and should be treated by the psychiatrist; it is a mark of disease rather than wickedness," Russell had decided in 1931.[41] He warned of the "deep-seated psychological troubles of envy or unconscious hatred, which may lead [persons] to take pleasure in the thought of war or revolution."[42] As he wrote in "Transforming Anger" (1934):

> In virtue of the transference of anger, cruelty, oppression, violence and hatred spread in ever-widening circles from the centres of power toward the circumference. Conversely, when those who have power use it humanely there is a gradual though slower growth of humanity in those who have less power. It is a mistake to think of cruelty and hate as inseparable from human nature.[43]

It is interesting that, for all his own struggle against anger, Russell was optimistic about its control in society. Had he forgotten his murderous fantasies, or did he believe that by bringing them to light they could be made manageable? His educational experiment from 1927 at Beacon Hill School attempted to educate for a warless world, but he had to allow that, as there were many "problem children," he had continually to intervene "to stop cruelty" (II, 154). Nonetheless, he went on warning about war and urging that reason prevail in its avoidance. He saw clearly that only by studying historical and political dynamics, beginning with the unconscious wishes of leaders and their groups, could the world be saved from ever more destructive armed conflicts. His psychology of warmaking is piecemeal and rudimentary, there being no sustained analysis of it since Russell came late to the theories of Freud and others. He should be credited, however, with seeing the necessity to shift from bland liberal Victorian progressivism into the tougher forms of analysis necessitated by the mechanized barbarities of our century which serve dehumanized political systems.

In "What I Have Lived For," the prologue to his *Autobiography*, Russell says that his life has been governed by three passions: "the longing for love, the search for knowledge, and unbearable pity for the suffering of mankind."

> Love and knowledge . . . led upward toward the heavens. But always pity brought me back to earth. Echoes of cries of pain reverberate in my heart. Children in famine, victims tortured by oppressors, helpless old people a hated burden to their sons, and the whole world of loneliness, poverty and pain make a mockery of what human life should be. I long to alleviate the evil, but I cannot, and I too suffer. (I, 13)

He does not explain why he suffered, nor are aggression and conflict mentioned as internal factors militating against pity. Russell was a flawed moralist, torn by love and hate from which he sought deliverance by impersonal service to humanity. Like many obsessional personalities, he was hyper-moral—forced by the war in his ego to be always vigilant lest he destroy more than he could create. As he confided to Lady Ottoline: "All my life, except a short time after my marriage, I have been driven on by restless furies, flogging me to activity and never letting me rest, till I feel often so weary that it seems as if no more could be borne."[44] Neither love, nor mysticism, nor service could entirely free him from the ferocity of contrary emotions, and reaction formation as a defense against unwelcome destructive impulses was an unsteady compromise. The legacy from Victorian moralism compelled Russell to do good to mankind, in general, but the ambivalent sensualist in him often did harm in actual relationships. It is a mistake to try to reduce the greatness of great men to their problems of childhood alone, but all factors leading to their contributions deserve study. We know that two other leading modern pacifists, Tolstoy and Gandhi, struggled against sensuality and decided that self-discipline and austerity were needed if nonviolence was to be a reality. Russell admired Tolstoy much more than

Gandhi, but both of them went to extremes of self-denial he could not accept. Russell's secularism thrust him into the age of psychology, which does not have saints in the traditional sense. By recording in letters and autobiography his struggles with inner violence, Russell sought to be understood for the imperfect being he was. He probably would have agreed that his social optimism sometimes outran his psychological mandate, yet it seemed better to preach hope than the reverse:

> In a war using the H-bomb there can be no victor. We can live together or die together. I am firmly persuaded that if those of us who realize this devote ourselves with sufficient energy to the task, we can make the world realize it.[45]

Exact formulas for reducing conflicts between superpowers trading paranoic projections are scarce in Russell's writings. It was as a moral pathfinder in international politics that he tried to function at the end of his life. Perhaps behind his optimism was the knowledge that in the main he himself had been able to control the very sorts of hostile impulses that darkened relations between nations. He knew imaginatively what nuclear war would be like, having lived a lifetime with such a potential in his own divided ego. Nuclear war appeared to be a form of despairing mass suicide, the personal form of which he often mentions as a way out of his intolerable conflicts. But as far as is known, Russell never attempted suicide, always trying to reaffirm life. In old age he preached the sort of "conversion" to a pacifist solution that may well have saved him from suicide as a young man. The habit of confession, of "always talking," no matter what happened, served him well. People with less turmoil, and capacity to reflect on it, are unlikely to see quite so clearly the perils of our late-twentieth-century situations.

Notes

This paper was presented at the International Psychohistorical Association's mid-year, two-day conference at Long Island University, December 7–8, 1984. Quotations from the first two volumes of Russell's *Autobiography*, published in 1967 and 1968 by George Allen & Unwin, are cited in the text by volume and page number.

1. Jo Vellacott, *Bertrand Russell and the Pacifists in the First World War* (New York: St. Martin's Press, 1980), p. 5.

2. Ibid., p. 26.

3. Thomas C. Kennedy, in *Intellect and Social Conscience: Essays on Bertrand Russell's Early Work*, ed. M. Moran and C. Spadoni (Hamilton: McMaster University Library Press, 1984), p. 223.

4. Quoted in Paul Fussell, *The Great War and Modern Memory* (Oxford: Oxford University Press, 1975), p. 8.

5. Bertrand Russell, "Why Nations Love War," *War and Peace* [later *International Review*] 2, no. 14 (Nov. 1914), 20.

6. Russell, "The Philosophy of Pacifism" (London: League of Peace and Freedom, 1915), 11–12.

7. Russell, "War and Non-Resistance," *Atlantic Monthly* 116 (Aug. 1915), 266, 274.

8. Quoted in Alan Wood, *Bertrand Russell, The Passionate Sceptic*, p. 103.

9. Quoted in Ronald W. Clark, *The Life of Bertrand Russell*, p. 339.

10. Russell, "If We Are to Prevent the Next War," *Century Magazine*, 108, no. 1 (May, 1924), 12.

11. Quoted in Clark, pp. 465–66.

12. Quoted in Clark, p. 467.

13. Russell, "Man's Peril," *Portraits from Memory* (London: Allen & Unwin, 1956), p. 217.

14. William James, *The Varieties of Religious Experience* (The Gifford Lectures, 1901–1902). (London: Longmans, 1952), p. 203.

15. Russell, *Contemplation and Action, 1902–14*, p. 42.

16. Ibid., p. 44.

17. Ibid., p. 70.

18. Russell, *Principles of Social Reconstruction* (London: George Allen & Unwin, 1916), pp. 5–6.

19. Christopher Farley, "Bertrand Russell: Reminiscences and Reflections," in J. E. Thomas and K. Blackwell (eds.), *Russell in Review* (Toronto: Samuel Stevens, Hakkert, 1976), p. 19.

20. Sidney Hook, "Bertrand Russell: Portrait from Memory," *Encounter*, (March, 1984), 19.

21. Robert Skidelsky, *John Maynard Keynes: Hopes Betrayed, 1883–1920* (London: Macmillan, 1983), p. 123. Hobhouse was a leading sociologist.

22. Russell to Gilbert Murray, 21 March 1903.

23. Russell, *Contemplation and Action*, p. 27.

24. Russell to Lady Ottoline Morrell, #399, 23 March 1912.

25. Russell to Lady Ottoline Morrell, #440, 24 March 1912. As the marginalia in Russell's copy of volume II of William James's *Principles of Psychology* (1891) show, he had a predominantly auditory imagination.
26. Russell to Lady Ottoline Morrell, #729, 29 March 1913.
27. Russell to Lady Ottoline Morrell, #300, 27 December 1911.
28. Bennett and Nancy Simon, "The Pacifist Turn," pp. 11–24.
29. Matthew Besdine, "The Jocasta Complex, Mothering and Genius," Part II, *Psychoanalytic Review*, 55, no. 4 (Winter 1968–9) 574.
30. Matthew Besdine, "Cradles of Violence," in *The Neurosis of Our Time: Acting Out* (Springfield: Charles C. Thomas, 1973),p. 86.
31. Ibid., p. 87.
32. Harry Guntrip, "Sigmund Freud and Bertrand Russell," *Contemporary Psychoanalysis*, 9 (May 1973), 278.
33. Barbara Strachey Halpern, *Remarkable Relations: The Story of the Pearsall Smith Family* (London: Victor Gollancz, 1980), p. 217.
34. Ibid., p. 217.
35. Clark, *Life*, p. 527f.
36. Russell, "On 'Bad Passions'," *Cambridge Magazine*, 1 February 1919, p. 359.
37. Russell, *Contemplation and Action*, p. 51.
38. Russell, *Power: A New Social Analysis* (London: Unwin Books, 1960),p. 202.
39. Russell, "Leisure and Mechanism," *The Dial*, August 1923, p. 115.
40. Russell, "For Better or Worse—The Choice before Mankind," *Daily Herald*, 7 December 1928.
41. Russell, "Are Criminals Worse than Other People?", *New York American*, 29 October 1931.
42. Russell, "How Science Has Changed Society," *The Listener*, 13 January 1932, p. 42.
43. Russell, "Transferring Anger," *New York American*, 5 February 1934.
44. Russell to Lady Ottoline Morrell, 22 March 1911.
45. Russell, *Portraits from Memory* (London: George Allen & Unwin, 1956), pp. 226–27.

8

Bertrand Russell's Sexual Politics

> It is above all in the realm of sex that early moral teaching does harm.
>
> —Russell, *The Conquest of Happiness*

As Russell's biography develops, we see in detail how his powerful intellect strove to dominate and control the pain of emotion. Russell was "thinking man" par excellence, an unremittingly verbal investigator of most of the troublesome moral and social questions we face, including sexuality and marriage. It is not generally recognized how much of the journalistic phase of his writing career in the 1920s and 1930s was given to the moral issues of male-female relationships. In assessing this writing, which often looks like propaganda for relaxing religious and social controls, the implications of earlier psychobiographical reconstructions of Russell's parental and romantic relationships become plainer. Russell can be seen as a depressive whose ego was organized by the obsessional defense which empowered his controlling intellect.

The following discussion shows that Russell's public teachings on sexual relationships, marriage, and child-raising draw upon his private anxieties and confusions, though these are seldom if ever directly acknowledged. Russell's public pronouncements are surprisingly disconnected from his anxieties as lover, husband, and parent. The confessional strain, so much a part of his earliest writings, is largely missing from the journalism on sexual morality. By the time of writing these essays he was so heavily compromised in his marriages and affairs that to explain himself would have been impossible. Especially

133

in America his readers had little idea of the turmoil from which his teachings emerged. Russell the journalist wrote not confessionally but as the "great intellect" tackling the day-to-day problems of progressive people who sought how to live better. The actual events in his marital history (marriage to Alys Pearsall Smith in 1894; an extended affair with Lady Ottoline Morrell from 1911; an affair with Lady Constance Malleson beginning in 1916; divorce and remarriage to Dora Black in 1921; divorce in 1935 and remarriage in 1936 to Patricia Spence) were little understood until Russell discussed them in the second volume of his autobiography (1968). This terse account is supplemented in *The Tamarisk Tree* (1975) by Dora Russell who remarks on Russell's aversion to "possessiveness" in marriage, and his preference for its "creative" aspects, which allowed bending the rules of monogamy.[1] Dora also mentions Russell's trouble with impotence, which should not be forgotten in accounting for his search for renewed sexual stimulation.[2] The painful complications of Russell's mistresses and wives, and their three children, were further disclosed in Ronald W. Clark's biography (1975). That Russell was hardly a disinterested commentator on marriage, but had a "private agenda," to some extent unknown even to himself, is no surprise. Are his essays on sexual morality, together with *Marriage and Morals* (1929), mainly self-serving, or do they advance understanding of our relational dilemmas?

In "Dogmatic and Scientific Ethics" (1924) Russell wrote: "The ideal to be aimed at is not life-long monogamy enforced by legal or social penalties. The ideal to be aimed at is that all sexual intercourse should spring from the free impulse of both parties, based upon mutual inclination and nothing else."[3] As to romantic love in marriage, Russell was skeptical, writing two years later: "If the purpose of marriage is romantic love it is evident that for nine persons out of ten a constant succession of partners is necessary, for romance is illusion and does not survive the intimacies of daily life."[4] These opinions were certainly "advanced" for their time, and we may wonder how Russell came by them. Should we simply observe that, in association with Cambridge and the Bloomsbury group, Russell was not so unusual, that he was acting from ideas then circulating, and that no psychogenic factors need mention? After all, the wave of emancipation from Victorian repression was just cresting, with Russell present to take advantage of new freedoms. He and his friends welcomed such iconoclasm as Samuel Butler's *The Way of All Flesh* (1903), directed against hyprocrisy in the Christian family.

In the 1890s Russell and his first wife, Alys, had revelled in Walt Whitman's poetic sensualism. Whitman's verse is mentioned as tonic in Russell's "Occasional Journal," though he reassures himself that self-analysis prevents "lust" from entering his romantic passion for Alys.[5] Some Whitman lines on muscular sexuality head up Russell's curious essay of 1893 on marriage, "Die Ehe," in which he canvasses the possibility of stepping outside conventional morality to indulge "freedom on both sides" in marriage.[6] Later Russell was to enter the Garsington circle of Lady Ottoline Morrell, where irreverence for moral convention was itself becoming convention. By 1915 Russell's affair with Lady Ottoline was all but over and he "sought about for some other woman to relieve my unhappiness," which led to the affair with Lady Constance Malleson.[7] Still accepting Lady Ottoline's hospitality, Russell remarks,

> at Christmas I went to stay at Garsington, where there was a large party. Keynes was there, and read the marriage service over two dogs, ending "Whom man hath joined, let not dog put asunder." Lytton Strachey was there and read us the manuscript of *Eminent Victorians*. (II, 27)

The prankster was the brilliant economist John Maynard Keynes, while Strachey's *Eminent Victorians* was the now famous attack on Victorian hypocrisy and pretension in the persons of such worthies as Dr. Arnold of Rugby and Florence Nightingale. Re-reading this book in prison in 1918, as a conscientious objector, Russell "laughed so loud that the warder came round to stop me, saying I must remember that prison was a place of punishment" (II,34).

More seriously, writing to Lady Ottoline in 1916, Russell remarks,

> I have read a good deal of Havelock Ellis on sex. It is full of things that everyone ought to know, very scientific and objective, most valuable and interesting. What a folly it is the way people are kept in ignorance on sexual matters, even when they think they know everything. I think

abnormal, and they suffer because they don't know that really ever so
many people are just like them. (II, 60)

Russell was reading Ellis's monumental *Studies in the Psychology of Sex*,
six volumes of which were complete by 1910. He further remarks to
Lady Ottoline that "it seems clear to me that marriage ought to be
constituted by children, and relations not involving children ought to
be ignored by the law and treated as indifferent by public opinion,"
adding, "the whole traditional morality I am sure is superstitious"
(II,60). This is much what Ellis wrote in the introduction to Volume
VI, *Sex in Relation to Society*, where he argues on behalf of women, who
have been put down by the Christian church, saying that the state has
a right to intervene in sexual affairs only when children are involved.
Broadly tolerant and humane in tone, Ellis appealed greatly to
Russell, who in 1933 reviewed the concise version of Ellis's studies,
Psychology of Sex: A Manual for Students. Russell commends Ellis's
"kindly sanity" in showing that sexuality is by no means the unvary-
ing ("normal") function assumed by many Victorians. He hopes that
legislation against sexual variance will relax, and confidently recommends "this truly admirable volume," even though its view of marriage is too conservative for Russell's own taste.[8] It is clear from his
essays that Russell was reading on marriage and sexuality much
beyond Ellis in England, books such as Westermarck's *History of
Human Marriage*, for instance. Mentions of Freud himself are scant and
superficial, occurring in such jauntily titled essays as "Are Parents
Bad for Children?," where the Oedipal bogey is given as a reason why
parents are less committed to their tasks than they once were.[9]
Nonetheless, the moral relativism implicit in Freud's teachings is
detectable in Russell's as in much Bloomsbury thought, although
Russell seems to prefer such English Freudians as the anthro-
pologist W. H. Rivers, whose *Instinct and the Unconscious* (1920) avoided
"the absurdities to be found in Freud's work, and still more in that of
his too enthusiastic disciples."[10] We do not need to add up
"influences" to suggest reasons for Russell's attack on the Christian
concept of marriage for life, in which the fidelity of both partners is
assumed.

In 1930 Russell was boldly asserting, in popular journals in

America such as *Parents' Magazine*, that not only was paternal feeling in decline, but that "marriage is tending to involve less and less mutual possession, and is simultaneously becoming more trivial."[11] These startling generalizations were founded on cases where there was divorce, something with which Russell would be increasingly concerned. His analysis of why the institution of marriage was weakening, for instance, in the *Jewish Forward* (19 January 1930), is based on changing science and technology, which in turn change social organization; but the main reason given has a personal origin. This is that interest in the marriage partner sooner or later declines, and sexual adventuring is used to renew interest. He hopes to see marriage as a union for raising children "in which the parties could remain good friends and continue to work together in spite of occasional sexual adventures." It is as if Russell were making quite explicit, with all the clarity of his famous prose, what had been implicit in the drive for sexual emancipation, dictated as much by his personal experience as by his liberal intellectual heritage.

The development of Russell's position is interesting. His Victorian parents, Lord and Lady Amberley, were advocates of birth control, and Lord Amberley lost his seat in parliament for sponsoring it. They believed in votes for women. Further, Russell's mother had once offered sexual favors to a consumptive tutor she and Lord Amberley thought should not die celibate (I, 17). Both parents were stigmatized by family and other members of their class for following the unsound opinions of John Stuart Mill. What to them was humane wisdom in Mill's "On Liberty" and "Subjection of Women" was dangerous radicalism in their class. With the early deaths of his parents, Russell could not have learned radical opinions directly from them. When he discovered what they had thought, however, he followed suit, much to the disapproval of his grandmother Russell in whose care he was brought up. Russell says in his *Autobiography* that as early as age twelve it appeared "self-evident that free love was the only rational system, and that marriage was bound up with Christian superstition" (I,38). His grandmother's "morality was that of a Victorian Puritan" (I,21), and he must have wished to avoid its unfortunate effects as seen in her children. For his own part, prohibitions of several sorts made him "unusally prone to a sense of sin" (I,28). Except for the mitigating but intermittent attention of his uncle Rollo and the brief, remote presence of his grandfather, Russell lived from age three until late adolescence with his grandmother, his aunt Agatha, and a succession of nurses, governesses, and tutors, isolated from his contemporaries and even from his brother, who was sent away to school in part because he was not considered a good influence. Granny expressed her distaste for sex, while Aunt Agatha was firmly under Granny's influence in a predominantly female household. It is remarkable that Russell himself had begun to see the disabling effect of such a household on a child who, forever after, depending on the severity of damage, would either reject sexual intimacy with women or sustain a specific relationship only for a limited time. As noted, Russell stated that his own limit was about seven years. Yet as far as is known Russell never directly addressed the reasons for his sexual ambivalence or for the impotence mentioned by Dora. While sketching in the factors autobiographically, Russell does not mention impotence, let alone recognize that in most cases impotence is traceable to inhibition of the sexual impulse by fear, anxiety, anger, or moral prohibition. There are, however, at least two statements showing that Freudian Oedipal theory was not lost on him.

In "Don Juan Has a Mother-Complex" (1932) Russell describes persons such as the philosopher Nietzsche, who fiercely denounce women, as actually being "submissive and terrified" by them. More perplexing are the Don Juans who seek ideal women—nearer to Russell's own case. According to Russell, the Don Juan is not especially manly; he is a victim of a "mother-complex," of a dedication to a false ideal in a mother who is totally devoted to him. He "desire[s] of a wife what [he had] failed to obtain from a mother."[12] But why the failure? Russell does not say, and the essay ends inconclusively, with a dig against psychoanalysts. He sees causes more clearly in an unpublished, undated essay, "The Break-up of the Home": "Mothers find it very difficult to renounce the power over their children which they have enjoyed during the early years. Freudians have accustomed us to the Oedipus complex. . . . Everyone knows young men who cannot marry without quarreling with their mothers, and others who cannot make a satisfactory marriage at all because of the hold their mothers have on them."[13] The operating word here is "power," maternal unwillingness to renounce control, and it is significant that he should remark especially on the old (such as his grandmother) dominating the young who have different lives to lead. Russell judges that, on balance, parents are bad for children. Does this merely reflect disillusionment at being a parent with Dora (he says he "failed as a parent" [II, 190]), or does it reach all the way back to struggles with his dominating grandmother who took charge after the deaths of his parents? My view is that Russell's sexuality was a damaged and rebellious result of multi-mothering at Pembroke Lodge, and that his rage against the feminine over-attentiveness of Granny, aunt, nurses, and governesses caused his reception of Oedipal theory to be eager but confused.

Russell applied Freud's insights self-analytically less than he acted out sexually ambivalent feelings about his granny and Aunt Agatha, trying in his writings to rationalize actions as a fashionable "new morality." Because he never gained release from Granny's affect-starved clutches, even after her death, he lacked a secure enough sense of self to stay long in a relationship with a female lover. Rage, guilt, and depression always worked their alchemy to loosen romantic ties, as is typical of the Don Juan or, more to the point, the Jocasta-reared genius in Matthew Besdine's terms. The homoerotic solution to this dilemma did not appeal to Russell, so he spent a lifetime idealizing loves which inevitably collapsed once he had encountered the real woman with whom he was mated. The pursuit of elusive love therefore amounted to an obsession, since love never reached its full potential however long it lasted.

The reverse of the "woman haters" he tried to satirize, Russell went out of his way to seek justice for women. In deference to his grandmother's social conscience, he actively sponsored women's rights, partly because he knew at first hand how great abilities such as hers were often wasted. This ambivalence toward the women who controlled him underlay the dichotomized idealization and then denigration in his marriages and affairs; it helps to explain the erotic mysticism, for example, found in the letters to Lady Ottoline, and the frequent cruelties to his women when love was over. This inconsistency of attitude precipitated a life-long moral struggle, which gradually resolved itself by Russell trying less to reconcile himself to traditional ideals of Christian morality and duty than to formulate a new secular convention assuming much freer relations between the sexes. The times were ripe for rethinking the moral code, but the difficulties of its reformulation were far greater than he could cope with, and most of the writing on the topic is unsatisfactory.

The beginnings are brave and sometimes eloquent. Russell's concern with fairness to women appears as early as 1894 in "Lövborg or Hedda," in which he argued before the exclusively male Cambridge Apostles that women should be elected to membership. Advocacy of women's rights took a more theoretical turn in "On the Democratic Ideal" and "The Status of Women," both of about 1906. Seen with "Liberalism and Women's Suffrage" (1908) and "Anti-Suffrage Anxieties" (1910), these papers give evidence of a strong urge to redress traditional wrongs, although we should remember that personal freedom for both sexes was for Russell a safety factor. As he says, "the recognition of legal equality would tend to produce a recognition of private equality, and this is an almost certain good result, since it tends to diminish the exercise of power and increase the appeal to reason in a relation where power is quite peculiarly odious."[14] Russell was especially sensitive to the danger of being "managed" in a relationship with a woman, though his argument is ostensibly designed to rule out the exercise of male power in marriages. The papers of 1906 remained unpublished, perhaps because their idealism had been so compromised by the raw actualities of the breakdown in Russell's marriage to Alys, as chronicled in the journal he kept from 1902 until 1905.

Equally important in thinking about Russell's later crusade for relaxed marital bonds is "Cleopatra or Maggie Tulliver" (1894), also presented to the Apostles. This paper seems to be about Russell's own struggle to reconcile desire with responsible social action, a topic no doubt pertinent to others in the society but especially to Russell as he contemplated marriage. Using literary examples of ungoverned passion, he formulates the problem of how to deal with passion, by which he seems to mean sexual passion, although as he says "nothing can be accomplished without powerful passions."[15] It is interesting that long before the advent of Freud's theories in England, Russell should warn against "the danger of too rigid repression of passing passions: in time our desires sicken and die: we become purposeless anaemic beings, saints perhaps, but totally incapable of any achievement."[16] Perhaps this sounds more like the poet Blake condemning "unacted desires" in the *Proverbs of Hell* than it does like Freud. In any case, Russell observes that unacted passion turns to rage and morbidity, so one must learn to judge how much self-control to exert without spoiling impulse altogether. The language is strong and symbolic, indicating how fundamental the issue was for him:

> No ethical theory is likely to have any permanent effect in the presence of an intense passion, so that the only hope lies in a correct psychology to strangle an inconvenient one in its infancy—but it is just in infancy that passions are often so alluring, and few people's estimate of themselves can stand out against such seductions.[17]

The difficulties posed in this essay are taken up in another, "Is Ethics a Branch of Empirical Psychology" (1897), in which Russell says that ethics should "investigate as best it can the nature and objects of our desire."[18] Since good must be defined by desire, ethics has the task of using psychology to understand desire. Unfortunately for Russell there was no psychology up to the task he set for it, and he found himself reiterating the problem rather than advancing toward its solution. He was well on the way to his final position in ethical relativism of choosing among good and bad desires. But desires are bedeviled by competing impulses arising from the unconscious. The only bulwark against wayward desires is reason, which governs obligations and preserves social cohesion. Russell knew reason to be a thin shield against bad desires, but he has little to say of the unconscious origins of impulses except that in himself they were extremely powerful. The evidence for this appears in his early confessional writings. For instance, the journal entry for 9 March 1905 laments that the breakdown of relations with Alys is leading him into sexual temptation: "I foresee that continence will become increasingly difficult, and that I shall be tempted to get into more or less flirtatious relations with women I don't respect." Those women he respects pose a lesser problem; those he does not respect, who yet attract him, pose the problem of causing self-contempt. The impulse toward this punitive and self-punitive sort of relationship alarmed Russell, who experienced it as "rather a mental than a physical feeling; it is a desire for excitement, and for a respite from the incessant checking of every impulse."[19]

This statement identifies the core issue in Russell's relations with women—his wish to get even for past manipulation and over-control, the imposition of power where a delicate balance between holding and release was needed. The passage suggests that Russell's sexuality was less passively neurotic than actively promiscuous, in which there was nevertheless a strong need to make good the incomplete attachment caused by loss of parents. Russell's obsessional relational style was therefore one of oscillation between infantile dependency and defensive control over the feeling that union with a woman carried the risk of control by her. This complex of feelings placed Russell among the sexual dissidents and led him to formulate an alternative moral code less condemnatory than that of the Victorian Christian consensus. This reformulation is surprisingly incomplete and full of unanswered questions. It is disappointing as an argument, and Russell would have done better if, like Rousseau and Frank Harris, he had written about his troubles with all their impulsive irrationality instead of trying to make it seem that he had fully reasoned answers to life's most complicated issues. Most of the untidy factors in Russell's human relations come out in the *Autobiography* (begun in 1931 after previous false starts); they hardly square with the confidently presented "new morality" of his essays and *Marriage and Morals* (1929), which should be read with these life events in mind.

If *Marriage and Morals* most clearly drew the battlelines with conventional sexual morality, its themes were not entirely new. Russell's arguments for sexual freedom had been anticipated for instance by Edward Carpenter in *Love's Coming of Age* (1896), but without Russell's bravura performance. The reception of *Marriage and Morals* was by no means negative, with much commendation for discussing urgent issues. However, occasional reviewers, such as Vera Brittain in the *Yorkshire Post* (28 November 1929), disliked Russell's advocacy of adultery, while the religious press criticized his anti-Christian bias. In America, where the reception was less friendly, Russell had already given offense through a lecture advocating companionate marriage given to the American Public Forum on 3 December 1927. Christians in the United States were much less impressed by the reasonableness and erudite tone adopted in *Marriage and Morals*, which, despite Russell's disclaimer, they saw as an attack on married fidelity. Where an attack on monogamous fidelity was concerned, no amount of appeal to the new anthropological studies of cultural differences in marriage and child-raising customs could exonerate its author. Bracketed with Dora Russell's *The Right to be Happy* (1927), which advocated sexual freedom for women, Russell's volume won condemnation from such figures as New York's Bishop Manning for openly offending against Christian faith and morality. It was his reputation as propagandist for immorality that dogged his efforts to teach philosophy at the College of the City of New York.

Marriage and Morals does not attack marriage as such, but it introduces a proviso about fidelity: "I think that, where a marriage is fruitful and both parties to it are reasonable and decent, the expectation ought to be that it will be lifelong, but not that it will exclude other sex relations."[20] To support this Russell makes a large assumption: "I think that uninhibited civilized people, whether men or women, are generally polygamous in their instincts. They may fall deeply in love and be for some years entirely absorbed in one person, but sooner or later sexual familiarity dulls the edge of passion, and then they begin to look elsewhere for a revival of the old thrill."[21] Then, as now, such assertions are far too bold, based only on Russell's authoritative say-so. The matter of instinct has been hotly debated in psychology, and even in 1929 Russell should have argued the issue rather than simply asserting it. Much in the book is open to charges of oversimplification, uncritical uses of examples, exaggeration, and melodramatic statement. Provocative, witty, and invariably clever Russell always was, but his iconoclasm, however reasonably argued it may seem at first glance, prompts second thought. The Swiftian brilliance of his attacks can be relished until one asks just what he is saying:

> If . . .the old morality is to be re-established, certain things are essential; some of them are already done, but experience shows that these alone are not effective. The first essential is that education of girls should be such as to make them stupid and superstitious and ignorant; this requisite is already fulfilled in schools over which the Churches

have any control.[22]

Use of ironic and tendentious statements, embedded in the most lucid arguments, is prominent in Russell's attack on the church and its teachings on marriage, birth control, and divorce. He is not above using false or unproven statements, such as that it is a "well-known fact that the professional moralist in our day is a man of less than average intelligence."[23] "The Churches" he lumps together as though they are of one voice in opposition to all sensual pleasure, and not a group with a common principle but many interpretations. It is unnecessary when arguing for the conventional wisdom of Christian churches, to point out how much Russell had to strain to counteract it.

In the matter of jealously he makes rosy assumptions that failed the test of the sexual freedoms to which he and his second wife Dora had agreed. When Dora had a child by another man, Russell was deeply upset and soon turned to a lover, Patricia Spence, who became his third wife in 1936. He had written in *Marriage and Morals* that "jealousy though it is an instinctive emotion, is one which can be controlled,"[24] scarcely a modification of his statement of 1926 that

> the Church says love should be controlled, but jealousy is the guardian of virtue and may be righteously indulged by an injured spouse. To my mind this is ideally wrong; love is good and jealousy is bad. The moral discipline which the Church has applied to the control of love would be amply sufficient to control jealousy.[25]

But the chemistry of human relations is far subtler than these statements recognize; whether or not Russell felt "jealousy" is less important than the fact that the birth of a child he had not fathered caused his feelings toward Dora to change, as had her feelings toward him. He claims in the *Autobiography* that the contingency had been foreseen, with divorce the agreed outcome, but he adds lamely, "I do not know what I think now about the subject of marriage" (II, 156). Having posed as a rational expert, Russell was reduced to a perplexity that reason alone could not heal.

Let us look further at the flaws in Russell's presentation of the case against fidelity in marriage. He argues the "all or none" response in his view that love is either spontaneous or non-existent. The clarity of his statements makes good polemics but leads to deceptive oversimplification when, for instance, he writes:

> I regard love as one of the most important things in human life, and I regard any system as bad which interferes unnecessarily with its free development.[26]

According to this, "love" is a romantic good which nobody should question, while systems are repressive and must be altogether bad. Repression of sex, he is certain, can lead to outright insanity. It is almost as if Russell were exaggerating Freud's argument in "'Civilized' Sexual Morality and Modern Neurosis" (1908) that neuroses originate in the sexual needs of unsatisfied people. But Russell is not primarily interested in love as sex, writing that "love is something far more than desire for sexual intercourse; it is the principal means of escape from the loneliness which afflicts most men and women."[27] These words touching on his own existential plight recall the finer passages in his love letters to Lady Ottoline Morrell and Lady Constance Malleson. Yet when sex inevitably enters into an adulterous relationship, it may unsettle and even destroy the prior relationship. Russell's chapter on "Divorce" shows that he was quite willing to accept this risk, and *Marriage and Morals* argues for a sort of serial heterosexual monogamy which includes marriage without being bounded by it. His words are: "Adultery . . . is no good ground for divorce, except when it involves a deliberate preference for another person."[28] Russell is far too sanguine about the efficacy of contraceptive protection, and virtually oblivious of changing emotions, as the experience with Dora's child would prove.

Russell was radical for his time. In a review of Durant Drake's *The New Morality* he condescends to call Drake "bold for a professor of philosophy" and hopes that his book will lead "to something less self-satisfied and rose-colored and more conscious of human liberties."[29] He accuses Drake of being too optimistic and not thinking through a "creative" and "positive" new morality. In fact, where Russell emphasizes achievement and individual happiness, Drake qualifies this with the caution that happiness must not be pursued at the expense of suffering and deprivation for others. It is this proviso which, one suspects, might be limiting to Russell's liberties. Drake's view is that "absolutely free love is too apt to be cruel" and that "divorce is necessary to weed out failures. But there should be far fewer failures."[30] Whereas Russell declines to examine the causes of marriage failure, which he treats simply as a fact of life, Drake suggests a need to look at the causes of mismating, a system of marriage counseling, and delays both before marriage and before divorce to prevent hasty and ill-considered actions. Russell's review inadequately reflects what Drake says, and its omissions are essentially those issues *Marriage and Morals* fails to consider.

The closest Russell gets to engaging with human failings in unhappy marriages is the popular article "Romance—And So to the Divorce Court!" (1928). This thumbnail sketch of the history of romance traces it from the chaste longings of Dante's *Vita Nuova* to the Victorian linking of love with marriage. Pure romantic love is an illusion that thrives "upon obstacles and separations," while married love is "based upon profound intimacy . . . of body, mind, and spirit, that breaks down barriers of self and makes it almost impossible to live another life as well as one's own." But married love can only endure if mind and body, indeed "all the elements of their nature enter harmoniously into their union." Russell, sees rampant modern individualism as preventing this, recommending that we look more at "biological factors, both in morals and in early education."[31] He says nothing here of love as the "anarchic force which, if it is left free, will not remain within any bounds set by law or custom," as he put it in *Marriage and Morals*.[32] Compulsive romantic love and sexuality were closer to his own truth, but nowhere in the popular articles are they discussed.

What reasons did Russell advance for men being unable to find complete satisfaction within the confines of marriage? He did not agree with Havelock Ellis that the need for prostitutes grew out of the orgies in which all societies in archaic times were said to indulge. The problem is repressiveness, and its remedy is that the sexual lives of women should be liberated so that the roving ways of men can be accommodated apart from prostitution. Russell cautions that, as most objectors to free sexuality are prudish and prurient, we should take the view that sexuality is as natural for health as eating, but not to be overindulged. He decides that "nothing but freedom will prevent undue obsession with sex, but even freedom will not have this effect unless it has become habitual and has been associated with a wise education."[33] There was certainly justification for advocating more freedom for sexual experimentation than the Victorians allowed, but Russell was never able to describe the limits of freedom, let alone demonstrate them by his own actions. This is an unacknowledged but major difference with Durant Drake, who was sensitive to the hurtfulness of unfulfilled expectations when one partner in a relationship moves on to greener pastures.

In general this is the difficulty with Russell's defence of easy divorce. He said correctly that the law as it then stood needed reform to allow escape where marriage breakdown had already occurred. The extreme cases he cites are when one partner is insane, alcoholic, or criminal—which supposes that the other partner is innocent and unimplicated in the difficulties. It is the simplistic view that marriage is an event rather than a process which needs to be questioned. That it is a relationship which, like other relationships, is either nurtured and given a climate conducive to development, is neglected and withers, or is undermined and dies seems to be a concept which did not interest him. In castigating those who question more readily obtainable divorce, Russell says that their real motives are envy, cruelty, and love of interference. But, as with most of us, it was easier for him to strike out against convention than to examine his own motives as a prophet of liberation.

Where children are concerned, Russell, in theory at least, took an altogether more serious view of marriage, which "forms part of the intimate texture of society, and has an importance extending far beyond the personal feelings of the husband and the wife."[34] Necessary for good child-rearing though he knew the family to be, he realized that it could not survive in its traditional form in industrial society. Some of the most astute remarks in *Marriage and Morals* concern the changing economic status of women, and the remarks on the diminished role of fathers and the take-over of child-rearing by the state have a prophetic accuracy. Yet Russell was not altogether unhappy about these developments which had, as their concomitants, some of the same freedoms for which he was arguing. The arguments pull in two directions. On the one hand, he advocates regulation of conduct, even at times "very considerable self-repression" by parents in the interests of their children.[35] On the other, he calls for "a degree of mutual liberty which will make marriage more endurable."[36] His hopeful words about restraint were written before Russell left two marriages involving children. Having himself been atypically parented, virtually as an orphaned only child, Russell knew at first hand very little of the usual ties of children to their parents. Nevertheless, when he writes specifically on the welfare of children, as in "Are Parents Bad for Children?" (1930), he is the soul of good sense and concern, but as soon as the child's welfare conflicts with the parent's freedom he becomes double-minded. It is clear which of the urges, restraint or freedom, won the day, and which would become the radical rallying cry generating more propaganda.

Marriage and Morals is easy to criticize for its hastily constructed and often opportunistic arguments, for its being a "potboiler." Mere opinion obtrudes in even its most thoughtful arguments; one wonders how even half a century ago he got away with saying that "women are on the average stupider than men."[37] Dubious facts and opinions abound as when he asserts that women derive no physical pleasure from suckling an infant, or that when a couple is infertile, it is the wife who is "barren." Unsupported statements are made such as that prolonged sexual excitement in youth without satisfaction is "nervously debilitating, and calculated to make the full enjoyment of sex at a later date difficult or impossible."[38] Russell can be excused for having no studies to back up his views, but this does not prevent him from writing with the force of unwarranted certitude.

Russell is on shaky ground, but ground which is essential to his cause, when he asserts that monogamy among primitive people is instinctive, that there are "traces of a monogamic instinct" still in civilized peoples, but that "the more civilized people become the less capable they seem of lifelong happiness with one partner."[39] Not to take him to task for his loose usage of "instinct," it does seem that he might have questioned whether something were not seriously amiss in "civilization," although he admits that it was the "economic motive" which first upset the instinctual pattern. It suits his purpose to believe that civilized men and women are polygamous, because who wants to admit that they are uncivilized?[40]

Russell's popular writing in the 1920s and 1930s on sexuality, marriage, and the family thus clears the way for sexual adventuring by making it the civilized norm. However much he praises its ideal state, the feeling conveyed is that marriage is a trap. As a psychologist Russell is deficient, having little interest in who traps whom and why; nor does he consider whether the trap is itself an illusion resulting from the inability to deal with intimacy. Russell, the cerebral giant, had turned his powers of thought onto the question of how the sexes are to relate. He had but one recommendation, "a degree of mutual liberty which will make marriage more endurable," a self-serving remedy that did not reach to the core of his anxiety about intimacy with women. Yet it can be said of Russell that at least he identified the issue of sexual ambivalence in marriage more accurately than had been done before. *Marriage and Morals* helped articulate some of this discontent and gave force to a "new morality" whose good and ill effects are beginning to be calculated, and whose wisdom is being questioned.

Notes

1. Dora Russell, *The Tamarisk Tree*, p. 156.
2. Ibid., pp. 208–9. In a letter to the *Observer* (7 Oct. 1984), strangely, Dora denied that Russell had been a Don Juan.
3. Bertrand Russell, "Dogmatic and Scientific Ethics," *Outlook*, 5 Jan. 1924, p. 10.
4. Russell, "The Institution of Marriage Is Here to Stay," *Jewish Daily Forward*, 19 December 1926, p. E1.
5. Russell, *Cambridge Essays*, 1888–99, p. 62.
6. Ibid., p. 70.
7. Russell, *Autobiography* II, pp. 25–26. (Further references to the *Autobiography* are given in the text by citing volume and page.)
8. Russell, "Havelock Ellis on Sex," *New Statesman and Nation*, 18 March 1933, p. 326.
9. Russell, *Parents' Magazine*, May 1930, p. 18f.
10. Russell, "Instinct and the Unconscious," *New Leader*, 3 Nov. 1922, p. 12.
11. Russell, *Parents' Magazine*, October 1930, p. 15.
12. Russell, "Our Women Haters," *Mortals and Others: Bertrand Russell's American Essays, 1931–1935*, p. 91.

13. Russell, "The Break-up of the Home" (nd), unpublished manuscript, Russell Archives, McMaster University, pp. 3–4.

He writes in *Marriage and Morals* that "it is not difficult for an unwise mother quite unintentionally to centre the heterosexual feelings of a young son upon herself, and it is true that, if this is done, the evil consequences pointed out by Freud will probably ensue." He adds that "if a woman is happy in her sexual life she will abstain spontaneously from all improper demands for emotional response from her child" (pp. 152–53).

The point had been made in *On Education: Especially in Early Childhood* (1926), p. 126, and is amplified in *The Conquest of Happiness* (1930): "When [a man] falls in love he looks for maternal tenderness, but cannot accept it, because, owing to the mother-image, he feels no respect for any woman with whom he has sexual relations. Then, in his disappointment, he becomes cruel, repents of his cruelty, and starts afresh on the dreary round of imagined sin and real remorse." Such "apparently hard-boiled reprobates" are driven astray by "devotion to an unattainable object (mother or mother-substitute) together with the inculcation, in early years, of a ridiculous ethical code" (p. 21). As Russell wrote in "Morality and Instinct," an undated and unpublished typescript in the Russell Archives, McMaster University, "One of the most important benefits which psycho-analysis has conferred upon the world is its discovery of the bad effects of violent prohibition and threats in early childhood; to undo this effect may require all the time and technique of a psycho-analytic treatment" (p. 8).

These passages suggest D. H. Lawrence's more dramatically realized insight into the sexually inhibiting effects of over-mothering in *Sons and Lovers* (1913), about which he theorized in *Fantasia of the Unconscious* (1923). Both Lawrence and Russell modify Freud's Oedipus complex toward a theory of the affect-starved mother who puts excessive emotional demands on her sons, the "Jocasta mothering" of which Matthew Besdine writes in his studies of creativity.

14. Russell, *Contemplation and Action, 1902–14*, p. 253. Russell's ambiguous sponsorship of women's rights is studied historically by Brian Harrison in "Bertrand Russell: The False Consciousness of a Feminist," *Intellect and Social Conscience: Essays on Bertrand Russell's Early Work* (Hamilton, Ontario: McMaster University Library Press, 1984).

15. Russell, *Cambridge Essays, 1888–99*, p. 95.

16. Ibid., p. 95.

17. Ibid., p. 96.

18. Ibid., p. 101.

19. Russell, *Contemplation and Action, 1902–14*, p. 27. A letter to Lucy Donnelly

of 19 Sept. 1904 discusses how one "wrong [step] is enough to do a great deal of harm."

20. Russell, *Marriage and Morals*, p. 114.
21. Ibid., pp. 111–12.
22. Ibid., pp. 73–74.
23. Ibid., p. 72.
24. Ibid., p. 114. Russell repeatedly tries to argue away jealousy when marriage partners indulge in other romantic relationships. A high-minded statement about "comradeship" between lovers allowing "liberty" is found in the chapter on marriage in *Principles of Social Reconstruction* (1916). Jealousy is vigorously attacked in *Is Modern Marriage a Failure?* (1930), a debate with John Cowper Powys in which Russell took the affirmative. In "Our Sexual Ethics" (1936) he argued that jealousy is merely a convention of seeing the marriage partner as property (*Why I Am Not a Christian* [1957], pp. 125–26). In "On Jealousy" (1931), in *Mortals and Others*, he urges men to change their views on rights over wives.
25. Russell, "The Institution of Marriage Is Here to Stay," *Jewish Daily Forward*, 19 Dec 1926, p. E1.
26. Russell, *Marriage and Morals*, p. 96.
27. Ibid., p. 99.
28. Ibid., p. 183.
29. Russell, "Reform Ethics," *Book League Monthly* 1 (4) (Feb. 1929), 213.
30. Durant Drake, *The New Morality* (New York: Macmillan, 1928), pp. 116, 115.
31. Russell, "Romance—And So to the Divorce Court!", *Evening News*, 20 Oct. 1928.
32. Russell, *Marriage and Morals*, p. 103.
33. Ibid., p. 228.
34. Ibid., p. 63.
35. Ibid., p. 186.
36. Ibid., p. 188.
37. Ibid., p. 83.
38. Ibid., p. 127.
39. Ibid., p. 109.
40. Ibid., pp. 111–12.

CHAPTER

9

Conclusion

The more I am interested in anything, the more I wish to
know the truth about it, however unpleasant the truth may
be.

—Russell, *Portraits from Memory*

Russell's flawed moralism compels our need for understanding because it is a powerful element in the early-twentieth-century liberal
attack on traditional sexual morality. The liberal attack on Victorian
conventions governing relations of the sexes was many-pronged.
Russell's writings need to be studied in relation to those of such
contemporaries as Edward Carpenter, Havelock Ellis, G. B. Shaw, H.
G. Wells, and D. H. Lawrence. Not pretending to be scientific like
Ellis, nor literary like Shaw, Wells, and Lawrence, Russell's reform-
ism bears a greater resemblance to Carpenter's direct teaching, as in
Love's Coming of Age (1896), though within the bounds of heterosexu-
ality. With less to hide than Carpenter, Russell stepped into the
public arena to argue against strict monogamy, and he found a ready
audience on both sides of the Atlantic. Russell's transformation from
sexual mystic in the letters to Lady Ottoline Morrell and Lady
Constance Malleson into propagandist and sexual politician signals
his emergence as spokesman for a new psychoclass.[1] That is to say,
the pressure for emancipation in Russell answered a widespread
demand for sexual reform in the intelligentsia and in the reading
public. The argument is that Russell's teachings about relationships
cannot be separated from his person.

To consider psychobiographically what Russell wrote as an
intellectual high priest turned popular moralist is to change perspec-

153

tive on those writings. His fame for incomparable feats of intelligence put people in awe of any opinion he might utter as a journalist writing for a livelihood. At the time few seem to have challenged Russell in the journals and newspapers for which he wrote on the popular problems of relationship. His self-interestedness was not detected, an air of intellectual distancing seeming to reassure his readers that they were being responsibly guided. Yet there is something pervasively unsatisfactory about Russell the popular moralist, stemming from his attempt to disconnect thought from feeling. In this respect he reversed the trend of the early confessional writings such as *The Pilgrimage of Life* and *The Perplexities of John Forstice*, where he seriously attempts to examine matters of mourning loss and marital obligation. For instance, *The Conquest of Happiness* (1930) facilely prescribes what no self-help book can deliver, a sustainable hedonism. Whereas in *Prisons* Russell had argued the Spinozistic ideal of religion as "union with the universe achieved by subordination of the demands of Self," the ideal of subordination of self in *The Conquest of Happiness* has a much less noble ring.[2] The latter book counselled self-abandonment, but not as the mystic knows it in the highest love of God. Russell simply urges abandoning the inner quest and ceasing from self-absorption to center on "external objects," and on pleasurable relationships.[3] Love is to be "adventurous and open-eyed" rather than bound by restrictive Victorian scruples.[4] He readily admits to an atrophy of imagination, even welcomes it.

> Gradually I learned to be indifferent to myself and my deficiencies; I came to centre my attention increasingly upon external objects: the state of the world, various branches of knowledge, individuals for whom I felt affection.[5]

Russell recognizes that the root cause of unhappiness is "a personality divided against itself" or, more specifically, "disintegration within the self through lack of co-ordination between the conscious and the unconscious mind."[6] My purpose is not to assess how happy or unhappy Russell was at any given time, only to point out that he knew where lay the truth of his own being, yet chose to abandon the imaginative path to it. Imaginative conquest would have been far more to the point than a "conquest" of happiness, which seems a contradiction in terms. The criticism would be unfair had Russell not worked so creatively in his journals, letters, and early literary efforts. Only the opening volume of his three-volume *Autobiography* lives up to the literary promise of his first confessional work, and even it is often less rich and probing than the correspondences from which certain letters are printed.

Apart from mathematics, which he acknowledges to have been an escape, Russell found his most creative act in his reflection on loss and sadness by mourning. *The Pilgrimage of Life* can be seen as a mawkish embarrassment, or as the courageous beginning of an inward journey to cure the disintegration of self. Why did Russell deviate from this pursuit? Was it only that the purple prose of this and "The Free Man's Worship" bothered him upon rereading it—the language of the unconscious having an unsettling effect? The language of "rational" discourse is altogether more reassuring, he might have thought, as he retreated from poeticisms. Philosophers place thinking before feeling; they are Cartesians before they are Pascalians. With English empiricism in his bones, Russell was loath to take the subjectivist's path toward re-experiencing in full the primitive emotions of loss and sadness. Bacon, Locke, Hume, and Mill were not subjectivists, and, while Mill wrote a memorable autobiography recounting recovery from depression by reading Wordsworth's poetry, he was unable to find a language fully to explain how he had become depressed. Could Russell, with his Cambridge and Bloomsbury connections, have arrived at a language embodying the deepest feelings while retaining the boldness and panache of his later essays? Would he have sacrificed wit and irony to a prose that linked surface and substrate as he wrote about the fate of man in the nuclear age? Occasionally, as in "Man's Peril," he brings it off, but the humane passions which engagement with the world had formed did not find a lasting literary vehicle. Russell's many books on public affairs which attempt to lift the discourse to a higher moral and even spiritual level include no masterpiece, no consummate statement such as Ruskin's *Unto This Last* that can be pointed to as Russell's essential message. Topicality was perhaps his bane, although literary immortality was within reach had he only been willing to accept the "madness" which makes Ruskin's career so upsetting to think about but so eloquent in its literary distillations. The inner and outer conjunction of forces never occurred as Russell advanced into the world from his moment of "conversion."

Self-division was the rule, as we have seen in the discussion of his remarkably perceptive *Prisons*. Russell dwelt on logical paradoxes, but it can be argued that the central paradox was his own being—the "divided self" of which William James had written and of which Russell was keenly aware as is apparent from his earliest writings. Bipolar inner conflict is the essence of the religious search that Russell began following the "conversion," a search now outside the confines of Christian revelation. As he wrote in "The Essence of Religion" (1912):

> The essence of religion, then, lies in subordination of the finite part of our life to the infinite part. Of the two natures in man, the particular or animal being lives in instinct, and seeks the welfare of the body and its descendants, while the universal or divine being seeks union with the universe, and desires freedom from all that impedes its seeking.[7]

This statement about higher and lower selves suggests the discontent of inner division. Russell's ego was weakened by incomplete grieving and tormented by obsessionally driven rage against those who sought in childhood to imprison him emotionally. Late Victorian and Edwardian literary language did not provide a terminology adequate to these feelings, and it was too early to look for a new language among the pre-Great War Freudians in England. While Russell says in the prologue to his *Autobiography* that "I have wished to understand the hearts of men," there is little evidence that he was looking in the right places. No matter how powerful the "passions" governing his life, Russell made himself too intellectually tough to examine feelings fully, as may be done for instance in writing and even in reading poetry. In the preface to *Lyrical Ballads* the Romantic poet Wordsworth had written of poetry as "the spontaneous overflow of powerful feelings," noting that "our continued influxes of feeling are modified and directed by our thoughts, which are indeed the representatives of all our past feelings." But Russell found no such balance, as evidenced by the disappointingly wooden occasional verses he wrote in letters to Lady Ottoline. Skepticism always held him from the release which poetry brings. In youth he resisted Wordsworth's assertions about immortality, holding them to be "of a vague poetic nature" and unable to stand up to intellectual scrutiny.[8] In late age he wrote: "My great hate is Wordsworth. I have to admit the excellence of some of his work—to admire and love it, in fact—but much of it is too dull, too pompous and silly to be borne."[9]

Russell's uncertainty about feeling is the crucial issue in estimating the worth of what he bequeathed to our culture. We may suspect that while he served a useful function as skeptic and rationalist with respect to Victorian cant and hypocrisy, he was also a rationalizer of inner conflict and anger. More was needed than to be rid of unjustifiable sentiment, which is why Russell's literary false starts are so regrettable. As a figure transitional into the fuller self-awareness of modernity, Russell with his razor-edged wit, unlike Shaw in theatrical rough-and-tumble, seems severe and defensive. (Shaw too could speak in ultimates as though judgment day were at hand, but he played it out in many voices.) Too brilliant to appear merely obtuse in his essays, Russell's literary fault is the one-dimensionality of affect the essays usually display. That he settled on the expository essay as his main literary instrument is a measure of self-imposed limitations on affect. The daring poeticisms of "The Free Man's Worship" (1903) were never again attempted in the countless essays of Russell's increasingly journalistic career. However many subjects he ranges over, the level, reasoning tone, for all the flashes of wit, remains just that: the discourse of an Olympian surveying the faults of human affairs and prescribing for their remedy. Were it not for the falteringly emotive early literary attempts, the sense of failed promise would not be so great. Yet it would be wrong to accuse Russell of not being of the first rank as a social and moral discoverer because he failed to clarify his inmost motivating springs, or even to acknowledge that they needed clarifying. He might have done much more, but also much less to explain himself. As a twentieth-century descendant of the Puritan confession, Russell's *Autobiography* is a remarkable testimony to religious and relational anxieties. Its incomplete self-explanations are not to be wondered at given the daring of Russell's themes at the time of writing. When they are published in full his love letters will help to bring out the proportion of self-understanding and humane concern to self-masking and narcissistic insensitivity. Thus judgment on Russell as a moralist remains ambiguous, contingent upon a skepticism about his teachings that he himself might have approved. Read in the light of psychodynamics, his confessions give insight into the dangers of unexamined emotion, however adaptive Russell's nuclear pacifism, for instance, is proving to be. Assisted by reading between the lines, we can extract from Russell's popular writing what is morally first-rate and of ongoing importance as we face the problems of war and sexuality in the late twentieth century.

Russell's conversion of 1901 when he was twenty-nine spoke specifically to the wrongness of war, a principle he consistently upheld through two world wars and into the age of nuclear terror. If we are beginning to learn prudence, to be nations of nuclear pacifists, then CND and the Committee of 100 have left their mark. But our safety will not be assured until we understand the irrational impulses to war in civil and military leadership, joined to self-destructive group fantasies in the populace. In his later years Russell strove to rise above political ideologies. The hostility of his own anticommunism merits rethinking, arising as it did in 1920 when he visited Russia and met Lenin. In the post-Second World War uncertainty of realigning power blocs, Russell suggested threatening nuclear war against the Soviet Union to hasten its compliance with international order. Russell had indeed been less a pacifist in the war against Hitler than he had been in the Great War, but to threaten a nuclear strike against the Russians does seem out of character given his later nuclear pacifism. The concept of Russell as an "angry pacifist" is therefore necessary to understand this lapse, together with his personal relations at the time, especially with Colette as Ronald Clark suggests.[10] Russell was not immune from anger as the outcome of fear and frustration, and showed the insidiousness of paranoic political projections. The meaning of the "conversion" is yet to be appreciated when he speaks of the "loneliness of the human soul [being] unendurable."[11] Astonishingly, Russell perceived the danger of interior weakness and emptiness, the fear of not being alive at the core. This is the "schizoid" condition of which recent psychoanalytic theory speaks, but which was opaque to Russell himself apart from describing the phenomenon.

The psychoanalyst Harry Guntrip writes of Russell's "conversion":

> I find this one of the most profoundly moving and revealing intuitive insights I have ever seen put into words. He discovered "the central fact of human personality" at the age of 29. Had he been able to follow it up with factual investigation, he would have created a profounder psychodynamic theory than Freud's classic Oedipal psychoanalysis. He had discovered what post-Freudian analysts were driven to probe and understand half a century later.[12]

In other words, in an act of deep and resonating empathy with Mrs. Whitehead and her son, Russell had discovered the schizoid core of loneliness hypothesized by Ronald Fairbairn, Guntrip, and others. Lacking the full biographical information, which points clearly to an obsessional ambivalence in Russell's relations with women, Guntrip was misled in speaking of Russell's core of loneliness "erupting" to destroy his marriage with Alys. Nevertheless, Guntrip was right in singling out the originality of Russell's discovery of the deprived and lonely primitive ego. Equally with Freud and Jung in their "creative illnesses," Russell co-discovered the nature of inner being with which psychoanalysis and psychiatry have since been working. As Lancelot Law Whyte shows in *The Unconscious Before Freud* (1960), from the Renaissance onward thinkers and writers have accumulated evidence for there being an active unconscious, but Russell's discovery was specifically of the empty, hungry, schizoid ego. While not connecting the schizoid core of being to his own deprived childhood, the implication of the *Autobiography* is strong. Guntrip feels that the *Autobiography* "arose out of his own deep need to understand himself as a person, to trace the path of his development to see if he could find out what had really happened to him and what he had become."[13] This surely is a moral act.

Russell, who might have become a great intuitive psychologist, chose the strictness of rational thinking instead, as English empiricism seemed to dictate. By putting intellect before feeling he failed to acknowledge that feeling requires critical handling by intellect according to the best psychological principles available. In general Russell placed himself above psychological theories, as in his critical remarks on the behaviorism of John B. Watson in *Education and the Social Order* (1932), where he tempers the approval of Watson's ideas in his earlier *On Education, Especially in Early Childhood* (1926). Even less ready to welcome psychoanalysis, Russell remarked with a grudging concession:

> The importance which many psycho-analysts attach to early infancy appears to me exaggerated; they sometimes talk as if character were irrevocably fixed by the time a child is three years old. This, I am sure, is not the case. But the fault is a fault on the right side. Infant psychology was neglected in the past; indeed, the intellectualist methods in vogue made it almost impossible.[14]

The suggestion of his own case is almost uncanny, and we readily understand the ambiguity of attitude in this statement, though analysts would probably agree with Russell that "character" itself is not "irrevocably fixed" at an early age. Susceptibility to depression and schizoid states, however, is established early, but would not be nearly so well understood until several decades later with the work of John Bowlby and others. Never especially friendly to psychoanalysis, Russell's verdict against its pretentions were expressed in "The Psychoanayst's Nightmare" (1954), a satirical story about Dr. Bombasticus's efforts to adjust Hamlet. As an analyst would say, Russell's wish to attack shows an unresolved hostility; perhaps in some sense he remained a Hamlet, as well as being Faust and Don Juan.

We now seem to be reversing the intellect-feeling priority, and acknowledge that verbalized feeling states are valid information and the stuff of useful communication. Since the advent of psychoanalysis and psychiatry, assertions of personal opinion on emotive issues may raise the question of why the opinion is being asserted. We want to know why people hold the views they do, and whether these may be contingent on unspoken assumptions based upon unresolved psychological conflicts. Rebellion against authority may be questioned as much as the legitimacy of the authority itself. The present liberal agenda includes psychobiographical criticism of the very emancipations which make criticism possible. In other words, everything is discussible especially when it has emotional content. Russell would have had little sympathy for the media world where everything is laid open, often without much clarity about the moral principles involved. Yet his own example helped to bring about the mentality that wants to probe into reasons for moral assertions. While forcing the pace of changes in morality, he managed to cover some of the reasons for doing so; we now need the complete picture of the man and his message. Seeing behind the defensive facade of pure reason, we glimpse the needy Russell who could not speak in fact or fiction of the full extent of his pain.

As his second wife Dora said, Russell remained all his life a needy little boy, a prisoner of childhood. Incarceration was a favorite image—"the passions which shut us up in ourselves constitute one of the worst kinds of prisons," he wrote in *The Conquest of Happiness*, long after first developing the idea in *Prisons*.[15] "Self in all its forms—in thought, in feeling, in action—is a prison; it shuts out the soul from that complete union with the world, in which true freedom consists," he had written in 1911.[16] In a sense, Russell's actions as a sexual being shut him off from the contemplation into which his literary efforts, however discouraging, had allowed entry. As a rebel against sexual mores, Russell learned to suppress the guilt which goes with "sinning"—guilt which he had once hoped would be transformed by forgiveness, as in "The Forgiveness of Sins," a meditation in *The Pilgrimage of Life* (1902–3). Yet over the years hardening of heart set in toward the women he hurt, leaving true feelings of pity and concern untapped in much of what he advocated in the public discussion of marriage as allowing sexual freedoms on both sides. The "free affections" canvassed in *The Conquest of Happiness* are not so free after all, a prison of self as repeated breakdowns of relationships showed.[17] In fact, the openness of the so-called "open obsessional," the most creative of psychological types, was all but closed by rationalization.[18] The defense against unwanted painful affect—rage against women who must be conquered and deserted—was never penetrated. Russell did not discuss his own Don Juanism, however much it emanated from the loneliness of the heart that had suffered childhood abandonment.

Russell wanted to teach the world to live at peace. The reasons for our inability to do so may be judged from his own hidden, unprocessed, retributive emotions about being imprisoned by women. He was unfailingly articulate, but using reason as a technique of self-sustainment did not advance his authentic cause in the peace his true self told him the world wants. Attempting to tell us about the good life, Russell was unable to articulate its hidden forces, the undertow of contrary feelings. Much can be learned from his example as we go forward in the causes he made so important and so real. Russell's greatest legacy may be his carefully kept writings, which invite posterity to understand him more fully than he could understand himself, and to build on that understanding so that his most fervent hopes for humanity may be forwarded.

Notes

1. Lloyd deMause, "Formation of the American Personality," in *Foundations of Psychohistory* (New York: Creative Roots, 1982), p. 106f. DeMause discusses the concept of psychospeciation, noting that the compulsive character belongs typically to the early modern period.
2. Russell, *Contemplation and Action, 1902–14*, p. 105.
3. Russell, *The Conquest of Happiness* (London: Allen & Unwin, 1930), p. 19.
4. Ibid., p. 38.
5. Ibid., p. 19.
6. Ibid., pp. 107, 247.
7. Russell, *Contemplation and Action, 1902–14*, p. 121.
8. Russell, *Cambridge Essays, 1888–99*, p. 47.
9. Russell, *Autobiography, 1944–69* (New York: Simon and Schuster, 1969), p. 89.
10. Ronald Clark, *Bertrand Russell and His World* (London: Thames and Hudson, 1981), p. 96.
11. Russell, *Autobiography*, I, 146.
12. Harry Guntrip, "Sigmund Freud and Bertrand Russell," *Contemporary Psychoanalysis*, 9, May 1973, 278.
13. Ibid., p. 270.
14. Russell, *On Education: Especially in Early Childhood* (London: Allen & Unwin, 1926), p. 31.
15. Russell, *Conquest of Happiness*, p. 242.
16. Russell, *Contemplation and Action, 1902–14*, p. 103.
17. Russell, *Conquest of Happiness*, p. 243.
18. See Andrew Brink, *Creativity as Repair: Bipolarity and its Closure* (Hamilton: Cromlech Press, 1982).

Select Bibliography

I. RUSSELL'S BOOKS AND ARTICLES BY DATE OF THE MATERIAL

A. Books

Cambridge Essays, 1888–99. In *The Collected Papers of Bertrand Russell*, Vol. 1, eds. Kenneth Blackwell, Andrew Brink, Nicholas Griffin, Richard A. Rempel, and John G. Slater. London: George Allen & Unwin, 1983.

Contemplation and Action, 1902–14. In *The Collected Papers of Bertrand Russell*, Vol. 12, eds. Richard A. Rempel, Andrew Brink, and Margaret Moran. London: George Allen & Unwin, 1985.

The Problems of Philosophy. London: Home University Library, 1912.

The Philosophy of Atomism and Other Essays, 1914–19. In *The Collected Papers of Bertrand Russell*, Vol. 8, ed. John G. Slater. London: George Allen & Unwin, 1986.

Principles of Social Reconstruction. London: George Allen & Unwin, 1916. Published in the U.S.A. as *Why Men Fight*.

Mysticism and Logic. London: Penguin Books, 1954. First published, 1918.

On Education, Especially in Early Childhood. London: George Allen & Unwin, 1926. Reissued in Unwin Paperbacks, 1976.

Marriage and Morals. London: Allen & Unwin, 1929.

With John Cowper Powys. *Is Modern Marriage a Failure? A Debate*. New York: The Discussion Guild, 1930.

The Conquest of Happiness. London: George Allen & Unwin, 1930.

Education and the Social Order. London: George Allen & Unwin, 1932. Reissued in Unwin Paperbacks, 1977.

With Patricia Russell. *The Amberley Papers: The Letters and Diaries of Lord and Lady Amberley*. 2 vols. London: Hogarth Press, 1937.

Power: A New Social Analysis. London: Unwin Books, 1960. First published, 1938.

Unpopular Essays. London: George Allen & Unwin, 1950.

Satan in the Suburbs and Other Stories. London: The Bodley Head, 1953.

Nightmares of Eminent Persons and Other Stories. London: The Bodley Head, 1954.

Human Society in Ethics and Politics. London: George Allen & Unwin, 1954.

163

Portraits From Memory and Other Essays. London: George Allen & Unwin, 1956.

Why I Am Not a Christian and Other Essays on Religion and Related Subjects. London: George Allen & Unwin, 1957.

My Philosophical Development. London: George Allen & Unwin, 1959. Reissued in Unwin Paperbacks, 1985.

The Basic Writings of Bertrand Russell. Eds. L. E. Dennon and R. E. Egner. New York: Simon and Schuster, 1961.

The Autobiography of Bertrand Russell. Vols. 1 and 2, Toronto: McClelland and Stewart, 1967, 1968. Vol. 3, New York: Simon and Schuster, 1969. Published in Great Britain by George Allen & Unwin.

Dear Bertrand Russell . . . A Selection of His Correspondence with the General Public, 1950–1968. Intro. and ed. Barry Feinberg and Ronald Kasrils. Boston: Houghton Mifflin, 1969.

Mortals and Others: Bertrand Russell's American Essays, 1931–1935. Ed. Harry Ruja. London: George Allen & Unwin, 1975.

B. Articles

"Why Nations Love War." *War and Peace* [Later *International Review*] 2, no. 14 (November 1914).

"The Philosophy of Pacifism." London: League of Peace and Freedom (1915).

"War and Non-Resistance." *Atlantic Monthly* 116 (August 1915).

"On Bad Passions." *The Cambridge Magazine*, 1 February 1919. Also in *The Philosophy of Logical Atomism and Other Essays.*

"Instinct and the Unconscious." *The New Leader*, 3 November 1922.

"Leisure and Mechanism." *The Dial* (August, 1923).

"If We Are to Prevent the Next War." *The Century Magazine*, 108, no. 1 (May 1924).

"Dogmatic and Scientific Ethics." *The Outlook*, 5 January 1924.

"The Institution of Marriage Is Here to Stay." *The Jewish Daily Forward*, 19 December 1926.

"Romance—And So to the Divorce Court!" *The Evening News*, 20 October 1928.

"For Better or Worse—The Choice before Mankind." *Daily Herald*, 7 December 1928.

"Reform Ethics." *The Book League Monthly*, 1, 4 (February 1929).

"Are Parents Bad for Children?" *The Parents' Magazine* (May 1930).

"Do Men Want Children?" *The Parents' Magazine* (October 1930).

"Are Criminals Worse than Other People?" *New York American*, 29 October 1931.

"How Science Has Changed Society." *The Listener*, 13 January 1932.
"Havelock Ellis on Sex." *The New Statesman and Nation*, 18 March 1933.
"Transferring Anger." *New York American*, 5 February 1934.
"Man's Peril from the Hydrogen Bomb." *The Listener*, 30 December 1954. Reprinted in *Portraits from Memory*.

C. Manuscript Sources

Russell's letters to Lady Ottoline Morrell are owned by The Humanities Research Center, University of Texas at Austin, with photocopies in The Bertrand Russell Archives at McMaster University, Hamilton, Ontario. The originals of Lady Ottoline's letters to Russell are at McMaster, where copyright is held. His correspondence with Lady Constance Malleson ("Colette O'Niel") is also at McMaster, as are photocopies of the early correspondence with Alys Pearsall Smith. Many letters in the correspondence with Russell's grandmother may be consulted in the Russell Archives, along with much other personal material as it is released from embargo.

Citation of letters is by date and, in some cases, by number when Russell and Lady Ottoline had decided on a sequence.

II. BOOKS BY MEMBERS OF RUSSELL'S FAMILY

Russell, John Francis Stanley (Viscount Amberley). *My Life and Adventures*. London: Cassell & Co., 1923.
Russell, Dora. *The Right to Be Happy*. London: G. Routledge, 1927.
————. *The Tamarisk Tree: My Quest for Liberty and Love*. London: Elek/Pemberton, 1975.
H. W. S. [Hannah Whitall Smith]. *My Spiritual Autobiography, or How I Discovered the Unselfishness of God*. New York: Fleming H. Revell Company, 1903.
Smith, Hannah Whitall. *Religious Fanaticism*. Ed. Ray Strachey. London: Faber & Gwyer, 1928.
Smith, Logan Pearsall. *Unforgotten Years*. Boston: Little, Brown, 1939.
Strachey, Barbara. *Remarkable Relations: The Story of the Pearsall Smith Family*. London: Victor Gollancz, 1980.

III. STUDIES OF RUSSELL AND ASSOCIATED WRITINGS

Clark, Ronald W. *The Life of Bertrand Russell*. London: Jonathan Cape and Weidenfeld & Nicolson, 1975.
Cooke, Alistair. *Six Men*. New York: Alfred A. Knopf, 1977.
Fussell, Paul. *The Great War and Modern Memory*. London: Oxford University

Press, 1975.

Guntrip, Harry. "Sigmund Freud and Bertrand Russell." *Contemporary Psychoanalysis* 9 (May 1973).

Heilbrun, Carolyn G. *Lady Ottoline's Album.* London: Michael Joseph, 1976.

Hook, Sidney. "Bertrand Russell: Portrait from Memory." *Encounter* (March 1984).

Malleson, Lady Constance ["Colette O'Niel"]. *After Ten Years: A Personal Record.* London: Jonathan Cape, 1931.

Malleson, Lady Constance. *The Coming Back.* London: Jonathan Cape, 1933.

Moran, M. and C. Spadoni (eds.). *Intellect and Social Conscience: Essays on Bertrand Russell's Early Work.* Hamilton: McMaster University Library Press, 1984.

Morrell, Lady Ottoline. *Ottoline: The Early Memoirs.* Ed. R. Gathorne-Hardy. London: Faber, 1963.

——————. *Ottoline at Garsington: Memoirs . . . 1915–1918.* Ed. R. Gathorne-Hardy. New York: Alfred A. Knopf, 1975.

Scharfstein, Ben-Ami. *The Philosophers: Their Lives and the Nature of Their Thought.* Oxford: Basil Blackwell, 1980.

Skidelsky, Robert. *John Maynard Keynes: Hopes Betrayed, 1883–1920.* London: Macmillan, 1983.

Thomas, J. E. and K. Blackwell (eds.). *Russell in Review.* Toronto: Samuel Stevens, Hakkert, 1976.

Vellacott, Jo. *Bertrand Russell and the Pacifists in the First World War.* New York: St. Martin's Press, 1980.

Wood, Alan. *Bertrand Russell: The Passionate Sceptic.* London: George Allen & Unwin, 1957.

IV. PSYCHOSOCIAL, CULTURAL, AND OTHER STUDIES

Berenson, Bernard. *Aesthetics and History in the Visual Arts.* New York: Pantheon, 1948.

Besdine, Matthew. "The Jocasta Complex, Mothering and Genius." *Psychoanalytic Review* 55 (1968), pts. I and II.

——————. "Cradles of Violence." In *The Neurosis of Our Time: Acting Out.* Springfield: Charles C. Thomas, 1973.

Brink, Andrew. *Creativity as Repair: Bipolarity and Its Closure.* Hamilton: Cromlech Press, 1982.

Bowlby, John. "Processes of Mourning." *International Journal of Psycho-Analysis* 42 (1961), pts. 4–5.

——————. "Pathological Mourning and Childhood Mourning." *Journal of the American Psychoanalytic Association* 11 (1963).

——————. *Loss: Sadness and Depression*. Vol. 3 of *Attachment and Loss*. London: Hogarth Press, 1980.

Bucke, Richard M. *Cosmic Consciousness*. Hyde Park, N.Y.: University Books, 1961. First published 1901.

Butler, Samuel. *The Way of All Flesh*. Ed. R. A. Streatfeild. London: Grant Richards, 1903.

Carpenter, Edward. *Love's Coming of Age*. London: Methuen & Co., 1914.

Curl, James Stevens. *The Victorian Celebration of Death*. London: Studio Vista, 1971.

DeMause, Lloyd (ed.). *The New Psychohistory*. New York: The Psychohistory Press, 1975.

——————. *Foundations of Psychohistory*. New York: Creative Roots, 1982.

Drake, Durant. *The New Morality*. New York: Macmillan, 1928.

Ellenberger, Henri F. "The Concept of Creative Illness." *Psychoanalytic Review* 55 (1968).

——————. *The Discovery of the Unconscious: The History and Evolution of Dynamic Psychiatry*. London: Allen Lane the Penguin Press, 1970.

Ellis, Havelock. *Psychology of Sex: A Manual For Students*. London: Heinemann, 1933.

——————. *Studies in the Psychology of Sex*. 4 vols. rearranged, with a new foreword. New York: Random House, 1936.

Euripides. *The Hippolytus*. Trans. Gilbert Murray. London: George Allen & Unwin, 1902.

Fowles, John. *Daniel Martin*. Toronto, Totem Books, 1978.

Freud, Sigmund. "Civilized Sexual Morality and Modern Nervous Illness" (1908). In *The Standard Edition of the Complete Psychological Works of Sigmund Freud*. Vol. 9 (1906–1908), trans. and ed. James Strachey et al. London: The Hogarth Press, 1959.

——————. "Mourning and Melancholia" (1915–17). In *The Standard Edition of the Complete Psychological Works of Sigmund Freud*. Vol. 14 (1914–16), trans. and ed. James Strachey et al. London: The Hogarth Press, 1957.

Freud, Sigmund (and Josef Breuer). *Studies on Hysteria*. In *The Standard Edition of the Complete Psychological Works of Sigmund Freud*. Vol. 2 (1893–1895), trans. and ed. James Strachey et al. London: The Hogarth Press, 1955.

Gathorne-Hardy, Jonathan. *The Rise and Fall of the British Nanny*. London: Arrow Books, 1972.

Holbrook, David. *Human Hope and the Death Instinct*. Oxford: Pergamon Press, 1971.

Horton, Paul C. "The Mystical Experience as a Suicide Preventive." *Ameri-*

can Journal of Psychiatry 130 (March 1973).

Inge, William R. *Christian Mysticism.* New York: Meridian Books, 1956.

——————. *The Philosophy of Plotinus: The Gifford Lectures at St. Andrews, 1917–1918.* London: Longmans, Green, 1941.

James, William. *The Varieties of Religious Experience.* London: Longmans, Green, 1952.

Jefferies, Richard. *The Story of My Heart: My Autobiography.* London: Longmans, Green, 1907.

Laski, Marghanita. *Ecstasy: A Study of Some Religious Experiences.* London: Cresset Press, 1961.

Lawrence, D. H. *Sons and Lovers.* London: Penguin, 1948. First published, 1913.

——————. *Fantasia of the Unconscious* and *Psychoanalysis and the Unconscious.* London: Penguin Books, 1971. First published, 1923.

Lester, John A. *Journey through Despair: Transformations in British Literary Culture, 1880–1914.* Princeton: Princeton University Press, 1968.

Lindemann, E. "Symptomatology and Management of Acute Grief." *American Journal of Psychiatry* 101 (1944).

Maeterlinck, Maurice. *The Buried Temple.* Trans. Alfred Sutro. London: George Allen, 1902.

Mill, John Stuart. *Autobiography.* London: Oxford University Press, 1968.

Morley, John. *Death, Heaven and the Victorians.* London: Studio Vista, 1971.

Nagera, Humberto. *Obsessional Neuroses: Developmental Psychopathology.* New York: Jason Aronson, 1976.

Pickering, Sir George. *Creative Malady: Illness in the Lives and Minds of Charles Darwin, Florence Nightingale, Mary Baker Eddy, Sigmund Freud, Marcel Proust and Elizabeth Barrett Browning.* London: George Allen & Unwin, 1974.

Rivers, W. H. *Instinct and the Unconscious: A Contribution to a Biological Theory of the Psycho-neuroses.* Cambridge: Cambridge University Press, 1920.

Runyan, William McKinley. *Life Histories and Psychobiography: Explorations in Theory and Method.* New York: Oxford University Press, 1984.

Ruskin, John. *Unto This Last.* London: George Allen, 1895.

Rutherford, Mark. *The Autobiography.* London: T. Fisher Unwin, 1896.

Simon, Bennett and Nancy. "The Pacifist Turn: An Episode of Mystic Illumination in Russell's Life." *Russell: The Journal of the Bertrand Russell Archives* 13 (Spring 1974). An earlier version appeared in the *Journal of the American Psychoanalytic Association* 20 (January 1972).

Spinoza, Benedict de. *The Ethics.* Trans. R. H. M. Elwes. New York: Dover, 1955.

Storr, Anthony. *The Dynamics of Creation.* London: Secker & Warburg, 1972.

Underhill, Evelyn. *Mysticism: A Study in the Nature and Development of Man's Spiritual Consciousness.* New York: Meridian Books, 1955. First published, 1910.

Vittoz, Roger. *Treatment of Neurasthenia by Teaching of Brain Control.* London: Longmans, Green, 1911.

Volkan, Vamik D. "The Linking Objects of Pathological Mourners." *Archives of General Psychiatry* 27 (1972).

Whyte, Lancelot Law. *The Unconscious before Freud.* New York: Anchor Books, 1962.

Index

Ada (nursery maid), 24
Amberley Papers, The (Russell's
  parents, 1937), 21, 43, 97–98
America, Russell in, 142–43
anger, Russell on, 128–29
*Autobiography of Bertrand Russell,
  The* (1967, 1968, 1969), 6, 57, 157
  anxieties in, 159
  on childhood, 21
  on "conversion" to mysticism,
    62–66
  on death and mourning, 46
  on depression, 39–42
  free love in, 137
  on governesses, 23–24, 36
  on grandmother, 99, 125
  on Lawrence, 122
  letters used in, 17, 97
  on loneliness, 85
  on love, 18, 95
  love, knowledge and pity for
    suffering in, 129
  on marriage to Dora, 144
  on parents, 20
  on Hannah Pearsall Smith, 76
  on Agatha Russell, 27
  "secular mysticism" in, 83
  sexuality in, 91
  suicidal tendencies in, 15
  violent impulses in, 120
  on women, 101

Berenson, Bernard, 37, 72–73
Besdine, Matthew, 8, 124, 139
Black, Dora (second wife), 6, 19,
  134, 138, 139, 143, 144, 165
Bowlby, John, 8, 32, 39, 42–44, 47,
  55, 160
Bradley, F.H., 77, 83, 84
Brittain, Vera, 142
Bucke, R.M., 77–78

Bühler, Miss (governess), 24
Bunyan, John, 38, 48, 53
Butler, Samuel, 135

Carlyle, Thomas, 9, 51, 52, 109
Carpenter, Edward, 142, 153
Chenskoff, 89
children, Russell on, 147–48, 161
Christianity, 82–83
Clark, Ronald W., 12, 17, 19, 117,
  134, 158
Collected Papers of Bertrand Russell, The
  (1979), 6, 11–13, 37
Conquest of Happiness, The (Russell,
  1930), 154–55, 161
Conrad, Joseph, 36
Contemplation and Action, 1902–14
  (Russell), 6, 37
Cooke, Alistair, 95
Copleston, 83
creativity
  "creative illness," 64–65, 115–117
  repair-loss theory of, 15–16
Curl, James Stevens, 47

depression
  Alys's, 40
  Russell's, 15–17, 25, 44
Descartes, René, 3
Dickinson, G. Lowes, 69
disarmament, 61, 62
divorce
  ending marriage to Dora, 146
  Russell on, 147–49
Don Juan legend, 95–96
Donnelly, Lucy, 73
Drake, Durant, 145–47
Dudley, Helen (lover), 6, 118

Einstein, Albert, 61

Ellenberger, Henri, 64–65, 115–16
Ellis, Havelock, 136, 146
"Essence of Religion, The" (Russell, 1912), 47, 156
ethics, 2, 143
Euripides, 54

Fairbairn, W.R.D., 8, 88, 159
feminism, 10
Flexner, Helen, 40
Fowles, John, 15
free love, 137, 139, 148–49
"Free Man's Worship, The" (Russell, 1903), 9, 40–41, 50, 54, 56, 69–70, 73, 83, 116, 155, 157
Freud, Sigmund, 8, 17, 38–39, 88, 118, 126, 128, 138, 140, 141, 145

Gandhi, Mohandas, 129
Gathorne-Hardy, Jonathan, 23
God, debate on existence of, 83
governesses, 24, 36
"Greek Exercises" (Russell, 1888), 70, 82
grief, 36–39, 41–44, 55
Guntrip, Harry, 8, 125–26, 159

Hall, Stanley, 127
Halpern, Barbara Strachey, 126
Hetchel, Miss (governess), 23
Hippolytus (Euripides), 54, 63, 66–69
Hobhouse, Leonard, 119
Holbrook, David, 8
Hook, Sidney, 119
Housman, A.E., 114
Huxley, Aldous, 102

impotence, Russell's, 19, 134, 138, 140
imprisonment
  of Russell, 115
  Russell on, 87, 156
Inge, Dean W.R., 82, 90

James, William, 17, 65, 73–74, 77, 78, 115, 156

jealousy, Russell on, 144
Jefferies, Richard, 72
Julian, Mother (nun), 105

Kennedy, Thomas C., 113–14
Kern, Stephen, 45
Keynes, John Maynard, 119

Laski, Marghanita, 72
Lawrence, D.H., 96, 102, 122
Lester, John A., 72
letters, 96–98, 109–11
  to Alys, 98–101
  to Colette (Malleson), 106–9
  to Ottoline, 101–6, 121–22
loss-repair theory, 15–16
"Lövborg or Hedda" (Russell, 1894), 140
love, 41, 95–96
  in Russell's letters, 103–5, 108
  Russell on, 18–19, 110, 147, 148, 156

MacCarthy, Desmond, 123
McTaggart, J.M.E., 77, 84
Maeterlinck, Maurice, 38
Malleson, Lady Constance (Colette O'Niel; lover), 18, 19, 91, 158
  letters to, 106–9
  Russell's affair with, 118, 135
Malleson, Miles, 108
Manning, William Thomas, 143
"Man's Peril" (Russell, 1954), 11, 61, 115, 155
marriage, Russell on, 136, 142–43, 144–49
Marriage and Morals (Russell, 1929), 18, 91, 142–49
mathematics, 4–5, 23, 81–82, 84
Memoirs (Morrell, 1963), 102
Mill, John Stuart, 71, 97, 137, 155
monogamy, Russell on, 136, 145–49
Moore, G.E., 84
morality, 32, 51–54
  of nuclear weapons, 62
  Russell's, 129–30

sexual, 91, 137–40
Morrell, Lady Ottoline (lover), 17,
  19, 35, 48
  letters to, 6, 18, 55, 64, 71, 78,
    96–98, 101–7, 121–22, 129, 145
  lock of hair of, 42
  Pilgrimage papers sent to, 37–38
  Russell's affair with, 86, 118
  Russell's "second conversion" and,
    82, 88
mothers, Russell on, 138–39
mourning, 55
  pathological, 42–43
  Russell's need for, 44–51
  see also grief
Murray, Gilbert, 54, 63, 66–69,
  119
Murray, Mary, 39
mysticism, 63–66, 74, 76, 77, 81–85
  Spinozan and erotic, 87–92
"Mysticism and Logic" (Russell,
  1914), 77, 82, 83

neo-Hegelianism, 84
Nietzsche, Friedrich, 138
nuclear weapons, 61, 62, 126, 130,
  158

O'Niel, Colette, *see* Malleson, Lady
  Constance

pacifism, 61–66, 69–70, 113–15,
  122, 130, 158
  in letters to Colette, 107
Pater, Walter, 22
Pearsall Smith, Alys (first wife),
  25, 135
  destruction of miniature of
    Russell's mother and, 22, 42
  failure of marriage to, 37, 40, 86,
    126–27, 141–42
  letters to, 6, 97–101
  Russell's grandmother opposing
    marriage to, 21, 31–32
  Russell's marriage to, 120
  Russell's separation from, 49

Pearsall Smith, Hannah
  (mother-in-law), 74–78
Pearsall Smith, Logan
  (brother-in-law), 38, 75
Pearsall Smith, Robert
  (father-in-law), 74, 75
Pearsall Smith family, 73, 74, 99
Perplexities of John Forstice, The
  (Russell, 1912), 9, 36, 43, 89
Pilgrimage of Life, The (Russell,
  1902–3), 9, 36–44, 49–57, 69,
  85–87, 127, 155, 161
Principia Mathematica (Russell and
  Whitehead, 1910), 16, 120
*Principles of Social Reconstruction,
  The* (Russell, 1916), 7, 10, 66, 118
Prisons (Russell, 1911), 9, 35, 47,
  86–87, 89–90, 156, 161
psychobiography, 7–10
psychology, Russell on, 143

religion, 27, 54
  "conversion" to mysticism, 63–66,
    70–78
  mysticism, 81–85
  in *Prisons*, 86–87
  Russell on, 156, 158
  sexual morality and, 146
"Religion" (Russell, 1903), 54, 85
"Return to the Cave, The" (Russell,
  1902–3), 52–53, 116
Rivers, W.H., 136
Runyan, William McKinley, 7–8
Ruskin, John, 155–56
Russell, Agatha (aunt), 20, 27
  36–37, 45, 109, 138–39
Russell, Alys Pearsall Smith (first
  wife), *see* Pearsall Smith, Alys
Russell, Lord Amberley (father), 20,
  21, 26, 137
Russell, Dora Black (second wife), *see*
  Black, Dora
Russell, Frank (brother), 20, 24,
  28, 36
Russell, Lady John
  disapproval of Russell's parents by,
    46–47

impact on Russell of, 101, 110, 124–25
Russell's ambivalent feelings toward, 139
Russell cared for by, 24–32
Russell's grieving for parents prevented by, 36–37
Russell's life dominated by, 45
Russell's marriage to Alys opposed by, 76, 98–99
sexual attitudes of, 137–38
Russell, Lord John (grandfather), 20, 26, 36, 46
Russell, Kate Stanley (mother), 20–21, 42, 97–98, 139
Russell, Rachel (sister), 20–21
Russell, Rollo (uncle), 27, 36, 45, 138
Russell, Victoria ("Toza," stepaunt), 26–27
Russell, William (uncle), 21
Russell-Einstein Manifesto (1955), 61
Rutherford, Mark, 71

Santayana, George, 2
sexual politics, 10–11, 91–92, 110
mysticism and, 81–82
Russell's, 133–49
Shaw, George Bernard, 157
Simon, Bennett, 65, 123–24
Simon, Nancy, 65, 123–24
Soviet Union, 62, 126, 158
Spence, Patricia (third wife), 98, 144
Spinoza, Baruch, 81, 87–89
splitting, 88
Stanley, Lady Henrietta Maria (grandmother), 4, 20
Stanley, Kate (mother), see Russell, Kate Stanley
Strachey, Barbara, 75, 126
Strachey, Lytton, 135
"Study of Mathematics, The"

(Russell, 1907), 4–5, 23, 84
suffrage, women's, 6, 140
suicidal tendencies, 15–17, 22, 44, 130

Tolstoy, Leo, 114, 129

unconscious, 159
Underhill, Evelyn, 82, 90

Vaughan, Henry, 35, 48
Vellacott, Jo, 113
Vittoz, Roger, 17
Volkan, Vamik, 42

Watson, John B., 17, 128, 160
Whitehead, Evelyn, 39, 63, 67, 78, 84, 125–26
Whitman, Walt, 135
"Why I Am Not a Christian" (Russell, 1927), 27, 83
Whyte, Lancelot Law, 159
Wilhelmina (Mina; governess), 24
Wittgenstein, Ludwig, 35
women, 6–7
Ellis on, 136
Russell on, 95–96, 101
Russell's affairs with, 117–18
Russell's feelings toward, 123
Russell's inconsistencies toward, 141–42
Russell on "mother-complex" and, 138
Russell's pacifism and, 127
Russell's resentment of, 110
Wood, Alan, 10–11, 21
Wordsworth, William, 49, 71, 157
World War I, 62, 66, 114, 118
World War II, 62, 115